I spent 12 years i
did not commit. 7
here now and able to share
with you is because I never stopped
fighting to prove my innocence.

Eventually, I won and my convictions
were overturned by the Court of
Appeal in 2000. I was free...but changed
forever. I knew, first hand, what
injustice felt like, looked like and what
prison can do to a human being.

I am scarred by my life experience but I
have not allowed it to hold me back.

This is my story.

Authoritize Ltd
16, Croydon Road, Beddington,
Croydon, Surrey CR0 4PA
United Kingdom
+44(0)20 8688 2698
www.authoritize.me.uk
Notorious by Raphael Rowe
As told to Chris Day
Creative Director Alexandra Truta
© 2021 Raphael Rowe
ISBN 978-1-913623-37-1 International Edition

Printed in the UK by 4Edge
Front cover photo: Amit & Naroop

DESIGNED BY

WHAT PEOPLE ARE SAYING

I am a serving police officer and your documentaries have really hit home and have really given me an insight into what it's like from the point of view of an offender.
Tony, UK

How you make us think between the argument of punishment versus rehabilitation of inmates is incredible. I really appreciate the rawness and I have so much respect for you.
Lent, South Africa

Another inmate I met and befriended was Raphael Rowe. He was a good looking half caste with dreadlocks who'd been convicted of the M25 murders along with some others. He showed me the papers regarding his case and also talked to me about it - I was convinced beyond any shadow of a doubt that he was innocent of the crime. It was blatantly clear that he was fitted up by the police. The witnesses in the case gave descriptions of white male perpetrators yet Raphael was still convicted. He was later freed on appeal.
Reggie Kray - In A Way of Life

Your work on World's Toughest Prisons has totally changed my perspective. I want to get involved with advocating change and rehabilitation like you saw in Norway! Thank you for asking hard questions and being so inspirational!
Marco, Norway

The insight into different reform systems in different countries is insane. You are one of the best presenters I've ever seen.
Patricia, Scotland

The documentaries you do are a breath of fresh air offering a unique insight into prison life all over the world, so powerful and fascinating to watch.

Marianne, France

What an amazing and eye opening experience you have gone through and shared with us, the audience. It's so intriguing and shocking at the same time. The fact that you were wrongfully accused and sent to 12 years in prison and that you are willing to go into the world's toughest prisons and give us a first hand glimpse and experience in that world is just astounding.

Rachel, England

I just finished the Brazil episode - when they asked you if you ever wanted to stop living during your imprisonment and you said no so quickly, that was a moment so inspiring for me that it'll hopefully be etched in my mind forever.

Natalia, Brazil

Thank you for showing what a fighter you are. Thank you for being an educator, both in the prison systems and cultures around the world, but also in the mindset you possess and we all should try to achieve.

Benny, USA

Thank you for documenting and questioning the truth behind bar's and the penitentiary systems around the globe. It's sad that it doesn't get that much attention by governments and the public in general.

Mila, Brazil

Raphael Rowe is like nobody I've ever met before. His journalism and storytelling skills are brilliant. He comes with a unique perspective and is a real leader. He was a brilliant mentor to me when we worked together and I always feel a sense of pride whenever I see the stories he works on. He helped instil in me a sense of making sure that whatever I work on, in whatever field, it has to be about making people think differently. That's exactly what he does.

Dhruti Shah BBC journalist and author of Bear Markets and Beyond

I hired Raphael to make films for Panorama and later for The One Show which is proof of his range. He is a story-getter, an authentic voice and passionate about getting the journalism right. He has much more to offer than we have seen so far on screen and not just because of his remarkable back story.

Sandy Smith, Editor, BBC The One Show

Raphael Rowe was a unique voice among the reporters on Panorama championing his own ideas with both passion and commitment. He was the driving force behind a string of sharp and timely investigations on environmental issues. He has also reported with great flair and clarity on the criminal justice system. He is a talented story spotter and was alone among the Panorama reporters in achieving a near 100% hit rate for getting his own ideas to air.

Frank Simmonds, Deputy Editor, Panorama

Raphael is a first class investigative journalist reporting for a range of BBC outlets including the six O'clock News and the Today Programme

BBC

Raphael is very very sharp, very bright. He has a terrific insight into all kinds of situations. As a victim of the justice system and its iniquities he is able to fill us in on the things we tend not to be good at. He knows a lot. He has a quite different angle from all our staff who come from middle class backgrounds.
Rod Liddle

Raphael Rowe served 12 years in prison for a crime he did not commit. He is now a reporter and an extraordinarily good one. He learned the job astonishingly quickly. He writes with great grace and integrity and he has an impeccable news sense. And he has that hunger for a story which characterizes all the best reporters.
New Statesman

Those struggling to get a foothold in the ever more competitive world of journalism can take solace from the story of BBC Panorama reporter Raphael Rowe
Press Gazette

Raphael, don't let the Daily Mail get to you - everyone says you're doing a great Job.
Greg Dyke - Director General BBC 2000-2004

Hey Mr. Rowe, I have seen all your work on Netflix and recently watched the JaackMaate podcast. I just wanted to reach out and tell you I am inspired by your story and can't wait for more of your content. I appreciate your realism and authenticity in a time when it is increasingly hard to find. Your fan.
Craig. UK

I can't believe you went through what you did and somehow became the man you are. I've been so intrigued about your story and how the country and the justice system let this happen.

Reggie, Australia

I have to say, the first time I watched the trailer for "Inside the world's toughest prisons" I can't say I was too eager to click on it - but boy am I glad I did. I have watched the entire series in one day and am overwhelmed and shocked at what I have seen. This is some amazing journalism.

Mark, New Zealand

The hope you must give to the people you meet in jail who may be innocent is breathtaking. Amazing work you do.

Lisa, Australia

I literally tell EVERYONE about this series. Any Netflix conversation I'm in I recommend it, and have never heard a negative review. Thank you for shedding light on that life.

Donna, USA

What you do is so important! Thank you for speaking the truth. Nobody should ever be silenced.

Elisabeth, USA

Your story and your journey are a true testament to mental and physical endurance, strength, and compassion. Thank you for doing what you do and for sharing it with the rest of us.

Tilda, Denmark

ABOUT THE AUTHOR

I am Raphael Rowe and my career was born as a result of spending 12 years in prison for crimes I did not commit. I learned about criminal behaviour, crime and the law from the confines of a maximum security prison cell. I transferred the determined questioning and methodological research skills I acquired in prison to become a respected and unwavering reporter who specialised in social and criminal justice. This is why I go into some of the toughest prisons in the world; people need to see what justice, injustice and reform look like around the world.

I have visited many high security prisons around the world, including the Democratic Republic of Congo, Britain, Papua New Guinea, Colombia, Brazil, Ukraine, Belize, Romania, Costa Rica and South Africa to name a few. Inside I film with some of the world's most dangerous prisoners, the guards, prisoners' families and politicians and talk to them about crime and punishment. Is it dangerous? Yes, it is, but I believe it is crucial to show an insight into how prisons around the World work. Only with greater knowledge and understanding can real reform take place.

My reporting and investigative journalism about prison, crime and criminal behaviour has significantly changed people's perceptions and I am very proud of that achievement. I left school at 16, and so my academic achievements have been limited but I do not see that as a failure. It is part of who I am and is testimony to overcoming the financial and social challenges I endured growing up in a deprived area scarred by racial discrimination and inequality. After all I went from there to prime time television and a career in investigative journalism that has taken me around the World!

I am successful in my chosen career because I am a curious individual, a skilled researcher, an experienced interviewer and a tenacious investigator of facts. I have overcome many challenges and learned to channel my adversities into action and energy and believe this trait is within all of us. Finding yourself can be the ultimate challenge.

This is why I volunteer my time to social justice projects I care about. Encouraging and motivating people to overcome their own adversities and achieve their own dreams is important to me, regardless of whether they come from a deprived background with limited qualifications, or are successful postgraduates, or just an ordinary person seeking inspiration.

The response of the viewers to my investigations around the World inspires me to continue with my work. People are curious to understand more about why people commit crimes, and the different responses and reactions of societies towards criminal behaviour.

This curiosity is something I have in common with the viewers and it led me to study a degree in Criminology late in life. It is important to change the narrative surrounding crime, criminals and the criminal justice system. A more transparent discussion about what works, and what does not, is needed in order to reduce both the causes of crime and understand the effect criminality can have upon both the victims of crime and society as a whole.

I would like to dedicate this book
to my Mum and Dad, my sisters
Belinda, Hazel and Joanne,
and to Nancy, Jay and Rosie.

"My love is unconditional"

ACKNOWLEDGEMENTS

There are lots of people I'd like to acknowledge who supported me throughout my time in prison. From the journalists who were able to convince their editor my story was worthy of publication or of broadcasting, to the individuals who wrote words of support in letters and posted them to me from all over the world. Those who stamped their anger on placards and attended rallies and protested on my behalf to those who supported my fight in spirit. Pauline Smith who came along and spearheaded our media strategy added some much needed energy to the momentum of our campaign and was solid support for my family who had not wavered in their efforts to get their son and brother home.

I went through a few legal representatives and do appreciate what they did for me in a fight that was tough and at times dirty. In particular Jim Nichol, Nigel Leskin, Trevor Linn, Daniel Machover, Susie Labingo, Peter Clark, Michael Mansfield QC, Patrick O'Connor QC and Ben Emerson QC. Their legal tenacity and patience dealing with a young angry me is commendable.

Without visits I would not have coped as well and so to Samantha, Jane, Ellie, Madeliene, Carl my cousin and Ernie my uncle, Pat and Mimmi my aunts and all my nephews who didn't have a choice Marvin, Alvin, Sherman, Shamia, Jamie, Joshua, Lewis and Simone. Your time with me helped keep me going and lifted my spirits.

My life was uncertain once I won back my freedom and then I met Rod Liddle, a former editor of the Today programme on BBC R4. Our unpredictable meeting changed the direction of my life forever. Sandy Smith, Jay Hunt and Stuart Murphy also gave me journalistic opportunities that allowed me to report with integrity.

My Podcast 'Second Chance' is all about moving on from mistakes, bad decisions or things beyond one's control. I fought to be given another chance at being free, it wasn't given to me. Yet I know without all of your efforts and those from too many to mention I would never have succeeded.

www.raphael-rowe.com

For Authoritize

Creative Director - Alexandra Truta
Editor: Chris Day
Editorial Team: Aditi Shah, Marley Muirhead
and Rosemary Day
Research: Elvira Uidila, Elvira Constantin

RAPHAEL ROWE
NOTORIOUS

CONTENTS

THE M25 THREE

The M25 Three were Raphael George Rowe, Michael George Davis, and Randolph Egbert Johnson, who were jailed for life at the Old Bailey in March 1990 after being convicted for murder and aggravated burglary. The name was taken from the location of the crimes, which were committed around the M25, London's orbital motorway, during the early hours of 16 December 1988. The original trial took place between January and February 1990, resulting in all three being convicted of the murder of Peter Hurburgh, causing grievous bodily harm with intent to Timothy Napier and several robberies. Each was sentenced to life imprisonment for the murder and given substantial sentences for the other offences.

The convictions were overturned in July 2000. All three men have consistently maintained their innocence.

INTRODUCTION

I've often heard people say that no experience is ever wasted. You know what I mean; that everything that happens to us helps to shape the person we become. My own circumstances made it difficult for me to believe that for a while. I endured twelve years in a maximum-security prison for a crime I did not commit. I spent every gruelling minute of it fighting to get my convictions overturned, which I eventually did.

Was that experience wasted? The easy answer is yes. But, without those very painful years, I would not have become an investigative journalist for BBC Panorama. I would not have been plunged knee-deep into danger interviewing a notorious drug lord in Afghanistan. I wouldn't have been chased down by armed republicans in Northern Ireland, unsure of what they'd do if they caught me but quite sure that I would not like it.

I would not have been granted the opportunity to film five series of 'Inside the World's Toughest Prisons' for Netflix. That experience gave my professional life new meaning; it became my job to give a voice to men who did not have one. These were just men, very troubled men, who found themselves in very dark places. Many had fully accepted the wrong they had done and that they deserved to do time. But now, they were made to exist with a live-or-die mentality, unsure each day as to whether they'd live to see the next, or if an impromptu riot might cause them to be decapitated in the night, their severed head serving as a football for their cell mates the following lunch time. The murder of prisoners took place in prisons across Brazil including Porto Velho Penitentiary, two weeks before I was locked in it to film the first episode of 'Inside the World's Toughest Prisons'.

My twelve years in prison meant that I was a lone champion of these men. Unlike many others, I could come from a place of empathy. These prisoners are people who made bad decisions in life and are paying the price for them, but they do not deserve to be dehumanised in the process. It is one thing to deprive a convicted criminal of time. It is quite another to render them defenceless in the face of the dangers posed in places like Porto Velho. It is my mission to use my profile and my privileged position as a journalist to ask those uncomfortable questions about what we want to be done in our name, as a civilised society. I know only too well that the criminal justice system is incredibly complex, and the administration of justice doesn't always produce the right result. Around the world, some countries do far better than others but the difference between those that get it right and those that don't remains vast. As you know by now, I'm no stranger to what happens when it goes wrong.

This isn't the part where I convince you that I'm a saint. In school I was disruptive and even got expelled. I grew up in South East London where it only took stepping out of your front door to start going down the wrong path. I single-handedly made my way onto the fringes of serious criminality. I mixed and mingled with the wrong people. I witnessed violent acts and wasn't too shy about getting involved in them either. The world I'd entered was one of trust, loyalty and making money. I was a criminal. I own that. There is no doubt that I was headed for trouble. But does trouble equate to being wrongly imprisoned for twelve years because of false accusations?

For myself and the people I mixed with, there was never a thrill from committing a crime for a quick payday or getting caught up in violence. It was about a community that had its own way of navigating survival. That was our unwritten code, and it was far easier to get pulled into that world than to be pulled out. I'm not one for excuses. That was the truth of it back then. There was the opportunity for you to walk away and make a better life for yourself. Without a doubt, it would take the right opportunity and often it wouldn't require much more than distancing yourself from that environment. If I had broken away or lived in a place where everyone was going to college or university, perhaps that would've been my ambition. But I didn't have any vision at the time; my life was all about thievery and my day-to-day existence. I didn't feel like I was being guided in a particular direction. All I knew was the world I grew up in.

My dad found his own methods to try and steer me away from crime. He'd beat me. He'd tell me I was headed in a bad direction. He'd even warn me that I'd end up in prison if I wasn't careful. I remember how he would say that in prison I would only be fed bread and water. My father's words served as a warning shot; they reminded me when I was getting a bit too close to the edge. My rebellious streak refused to be smudged out so easily. I can't deny the parallels between my father's warnings and the course my life took. But who's to say what would've happened if I hadn't been taken in on the 19th of December 1988, the day of that horrendous arrest? If I hadn't been wrongly convicted, the very next day I could have met someone who turned my life around. I was not a silly guy. I was just young and naïve. I had no sympathy, no empathy, nor any of those traits that you develop as you get older. How was I any different from any other twenty-year-old?

Imprisonment could not deny me my formative years. I grew, defiant of my circumstances, like a stem of green that stretched to the sun through cracked slabs of concrete. Prison reshaped my life and my perspective. I learned what torture was. I never knew if I would ever be released. Spending my life locked in an eight-by-ten cell would have broken me at some point. My body was subject to abuse. The amount of time I spent in segregation, stripped naked and beaten by prison officers could have crushed my spirit and soul. But I couldn't dare allow it to. There is a shift that happens when you enter your cell for the first time and the door shuts. People react very differently; every prisoner develops their coping mechanism. The guilty tend to be more accepting. I've sat down with many guilty men and the second their cell door closes their fate is sealed. My reaction became my driving force. I mustered that inner strength we all have in us when we need it most. Prison didn't make me. My inner workings, my mind and my determination did. I did that.

Many have compared the self-isolation and quarantine that COVID19 demands from us to the experience of being in prison. It's not even close. That's not to undermine the hardship and isolation that COVID19 has inflicted on many. But they are wrong. Outside we have our freedom. We can look out of the window and see life moving before our eyes, a luxury I'm sure you would recognise if it were taken from you. We can move around in our houses or flats. We can interact with our loved ones even if it is through a pane of glass or a screen. Sure, we've been given government guidelines as to what we can and can't do. But we can walk out of that door anytime we want to. In prison, only one side of the door has a handle and it's the outside. You wait forever until someone comes to tell you what to do and show you where you can go. Outside, you can make choices. No prisoner is handed that privilege. So much is taken from you physically that you can't help but start to feel the psychological impact. Being imprisoned requires a completely different mindset. You develop different ways to cope. My methods evolved into a skill-set.

I became a very visual person and I gained a better understanding of men. You can imagine that prison is quite the melting pot. On a daily basis I was rubbing elbows with men of all different sizes all posing different levels of risk. They could act hard or they could be alright. Some were manipulative. Some were conniving. Some posed a daily threat. It was my job to keep myself breathing. Those daily interactions around such a collection of different traits taught me how to read a man. It doesn't have to be as blatant as a knife in his hand or an expression on his face. It's an instinct, not a science, a by-product of having to constantly be hyper aware of your environment. That instinct has served me well, especially as a journalist.

Still, you could've told me that prison would lead me to the life I have now, and I still wouldn't wish to do a day of it. It would be a lie to say that this gross misfortune did not open the doors to the life that I am fortunate to lead now. But no-one should spend a day, a week, a month, a minute in prison for something they did not do. Even if I put aside the fact that I had been wrongfully imprisoned, there still stirred deep within me as a young man the feeling that I did not belong in that cell. I needed to be free again. Literally. Metaphorically. Desperately. I turned the bitter hatred inside of me into fuel for the fight for my release. So, let me take you on the journey from the beginning.

01

THE SON
AND BROTHER

" MY FATHER'S WORDS
SERVED AS A WARNING
SHOT; THEY REMINDED ME
WHEN I WAS GETTING TOO
CLOSE TO THE EDGE. "

CHAPTER 1

Son and Brother

My story starts in South East London. I was raised under the sound of Bow Bells surrounded by bustling working-class communities. After giving birth to my three older sisters in hospital beds, my mum craved the comfort of her own home by the time it came round to me. I was born in 1968 in Flat 34 Shelley House where we stayed until I was three. It stood in King and Queen Street, just round the corner from East Street market on Walworth Road and opposite the old Labour Party Headquarters. When she was about five years old my middle sister, Hazel, knocked over the paraffin heater that we used to warm the flat. No one was hurt but the damage from the smoke and the fumes blew us into a new home; 12 Guildford House on the Crawford Estate in Camberwell Green.

Back then, council estates weren't just similar in how they looked but also the people they housed. Like our old place, Guildford House was what you would call 'colourful'. It was home to a real mix of families; Scottish families, Irish Families, mixed-race families, black and white families, Chinese families, almost any other ethnicity you could imagine. The one thing we all had in common was that we were all low-income and working class. But that was our glue; it was a real community with us all looking out for each other. There was no real tension back then. If there was it went over my head as a kid. We were all friends with a common purpose of surviving and just getting through the day. It was never quiet. My childhood there was sound tracked with

25

a mixtape of gossip, fights and people screaming at each other. It was life as we knew it.

My dad is Jamaican and is also called Raphael. Once his brother Alvin – already settled in England – had enough money to support them both, my twenty-six year old father set sail for Southampton. Coming to England, or 'The Motherland' as Jamaicans call it, must have been quite the adventure for him. My dad had a tough upbringing. His mother died soon after his birth so parenthood was left to my grandfather. From what I heard on a trip I made to Jamaica at age thirty-two, he was hard on my dad and his siblings. My uncle and father found work in the building trade and quickly settled down to a comfortable life. That's when he met my mother, Rosemary Prior. The two of them were lucky enough to experience the original vibrant scene of Ladbroke Grove back in the 60s.

My dad met my mum when she was sixteen. Born and bred in London, she was still at school and living with my grandparents and older brother and sister, Ernie and Pat, in Shepherds Bush. Although her parents weren't too keen on her marrying a black man from Jamaica they gave up fighting when she hit seventeen. My mum was so young when she married my dad; I have a sneaky suspicion it was because she was already pregnant with my eldest sister, Belinda. From memory, the relationship between my mum and dad was never particularly open or affectionate. But their marriage had a strength you'd find hard to match these days. My dad is an old school kind of Jamaican. The day he stepped foot in this country he was dressed to the nines in his classic combo: a trilby, suit and a tie that sat dead straight down his chest. He still dons that look to this day. His hair would be greased with Brylcreem and when he walked past a waft of Old Spice or Brut aftershave would dance its way up your nose. My dad's measured and immaculate appearance stood in stark contrast to his explosive and unpredictable temper. More than once did I witness him hit my mum. Although she would scream at him and fight back she was no match for his aggression. There were times when the neighbours called the police but before they'd had a chance to switch on their sirens my parents would be made up, happy as Larry like nothing had happened. They've now been together for fifty-seven years.

That kind of volatility was traumatising to both me and my sisters. You never knew where you stood. One minute we'd be going about our daily lives and the next we'd find ourselves the targets of his explosive temper. Sometimes it was fuelled by anger and at other times it was parental discipline gone a step too far. His cruelty brewed hatred in me towards him: I could never understand why he acted so. It is only now with adult eyes that I can see that it was his way – however flawed – of guiding his children's behaviour.

I think my dad struggled to fully settle into Britain. Back home in Jamaica, duties on his father's farmland kept him far away from any kind of formal education. When he got here, unable to read and write, he remained drawn to his fellow countrymen. You would always find my dad and his friends at one of those basement house parties. Ska and reggae would boom through the floorboards and make them shimmy with the rhythm. Liquor flowed from hand to hand, lip to lip. Cigarette smoke and a sweet sweat mingled above the heads of dancing couples, hips rocking low and steady as if the air was as thick as black treacle. Freed momentarily from the burden of British-English, the men would flex their tongues with patois to charm the ladies. As a boy you'd stow away their words ready to impress the next girl who caught your eye. They were the kind of nights that as a kid, made you desperate to grow up. The vibe that came with Caribbean music is one of my clearest memories of those days alongside dancing and drinking.

My dad has always been a drinker. His drink of choice was either Tennents' Lager or Special Brew, a beer so strong it would do more than put hairs on your chest. White rum – the devil's water – was always somewhere to be found amongst other spirits floating around in our house. In fact, it was alcohol that led to the sale of my dad's car. He owned a 1960 Morris Oxford. If you asked us now, my sister, Joanne, and I could still recite the registration: UPK 679F. I couldn't tell you why we remember it but we've just never forgotten. That car was kissed goodbye when my dad got banned for drink-driving more than once. Apart from that, I don't believe he ever fell into trouble with the law.

My mum was a housewife for the most part. It wasn't until my sisters were much older that she had the time to work as a cleaner at Guy's Hospital as she would have been doing most of the cooking in the house. Both my parents, though, were great cooks. We'd have Jamaican food, English food and sometimes a mixture of both. I loved them equally, never once thinking to pick a favourite between chicken with rice and peas and a Sunday Roast. Both dishes are up there with the corned-beef hash dish my mum used to make that takes me right back to my childhood. We never had much money as a family but we did eat well.

Beneath the surface, my mum was a strong woman. You would have to be to first give birth to four children in succession and then bring them up with very little help or financial means. She would keep us fed, our house clean and get us to and from school every day. She'd have to drag us around shopping and deal with our daily demands, and she managed all of this without

28

ever complaining. I was her youngest child and she was just a young woman in her twenties when I came along. I have such a profound admiration for my mum and I could never forgive myself for the pain and suffering that my behaviour brought to her door.

Once, after work, my mum came home with an action figure of Steve Austin: The Six Million Dollar Bionic Man. It was from my favourite TV show so instantly that toy became the prized piece amongst my humble collection of action figures. Before Steve Austin, I had a handful of Action Man toys whose eyes could move from side to side from the backs of their heads. To me they were the coolest thing since sliced bread and I played with them all the time. What made them really special was that they were a present from my mother. According to my sisters I got special treatment.

Being the only boy, they'd tease me for being spoilt or being allowed to get away with so much. I had my own room while my three sisters had to share one. At one point my parents saved up enough money to buy me a bright yellow racing bike. I was fiercely proud of that bike, always zipping about with it. But it was the same as the Steve Austin action figure: it was special because of the sacrifices they made to get it for me. Between a labourer father and a housewife mother with an occasional cleaning job, we never did have that much money around. My sisters and I never really got pocket money. When my dad's friends came round for a drink and I was sent to pick up beer from the shop, I might have got lucky and been able to keep the change. This was only ever enough to buy a Curly Wurly or a lollipop. This meant that bike and that action figure meant the world.

Despite a challenging upbringing, my parents did do things to show their love for me and my sisters, albeit rarely with words.

One of the adventures my dad would take me on was a trip to Spitalfields Market. We would go to bulk buy meat to store in our freezer. I'd wake up at three in the morning, buzzed to be up at such a grown-up time. I'd sit on the bus ride to the market seeing London as the sunrise just started to peep through the buildings. Beyond that, I did very little with my father as a child. I couldn't hold it against him; it was not part of his own upbringing. I did get a pang of jealousy when I realised other people got to do more things with their dads than I did. The first and only football game I ever went to as a child was with a kid from our estate and his dad. I was footie-mad by then. In front of our block of flats was a fenced island of grass with do-not-trespass signs stretched across it. To us it was our own private, one-of-a-kind professional football pitch and we scored afternoons into our memories with the games we'd play on that makeshift little patch. Sometimes it would be just me and another boy playing end-to-end goalie. We'd make two opposing goals with tree twigs stuck in the ground and try to score past each other on the length of the pitch. We'd pretend to be our favourite players who'd dribbled across our screens on that weekend's 'Match of the Day' TV programme. All the men I saw on TV became my inspiration. I wanted to be like Liam Brady who was a left-footed player for Arsenal at the time. I wanted to be like George Best or John Conte, the middleweight boxer, or Muhammed Ali – the greatest word-smith of them all. Michael Jackson and James Brown were probably the first black musicians I ever saw on television.

They were the people with success stories that were a million miles away from my reality.

Our football games would be whistled off - at least for me - by my mum's call for tea. I used to dread it. But right on her command I would march up the block of flats' stairs to my front door, covered in mud and hot and thirsty. I'd whip open the fridge and drink the first cold thing my eyes landed on. Sometimes it would be an open can of my dad's beer or lager. I'd sleep well after that thinking it was exhaustion. Most times I could rely on the large container of Sarsaparilla that was always in our house. It was my favourite drink. This purple coloured bitter-sweet soft drink needed diluting with water and almost every kid on the estate drank it. You used to be able to get it from a kiosk at Walworth Road market. Though I haven't had a glass for many, many years, I think you could still find it there if you tried.

Those days playing football were some of the best in my childhood. Playing with mates without a care in the world was my utopia. This wasn't to be the only way football played a part in my life. I was an athletic boy and good at sports. Once, when I was older, the Metropolitan Police football team asked me to join their local club. My dad wouldn't let me. Granted, it was while I was grounded for having got into trouble with the police. I know, the irony. But it felt like one extra twist in my life that made up a string of events where I felt my father didn't support me. I don't remember him being very encouraging or supporting me in any of the things I wanted to do or that I was good at. I know that's my perspective and it's how I remember it.

It was now 1979 and I was eleven years old. I remember being woken up by my father arriving home after one of his drinking binges at two o'clock in the morning. He told me to get up and get dressed. Before I could rub the sleep from my eyes we were at what was to become our new home a few miles up the road at 28 Grimsel Path, just off Camberwell New Road.

31

This new council property was larger, had three floors and had it's very own staircase! It boasted a small fenced garden at the back with a small patch of grass at the front. It had one more bedroom than our flat at Guildford House which meant that Belinda, the eldest, got her own room for the first time when we moved in a few days later.

Sport was one of the other things my father and I disagreed on. Frustratingly, he preferred to watch a movie on Saturday evening, which quashed any chance of me catching 'Match Of The Day'. You couldn't record a programme or find it on catch-up TV back then. We only had one small TV in the front room so the radio became my way to tune into the game. My father did like the horses. Everyday he would visit the bookies to place his bets. He never won much and I dread to think on how much he lost over the years. The only game he really loved was cricket

As I mentioned, father-son outings were a rare event in my childhood. He did once take me and a friend nicknamed 'Stix' to Notting Hill Carnival. It was an eye opener. A few years later I would go again with a gang of mates being boisterous and causing mayhem. I was at the age where you think you run the world and nothing can stand in your way. Our new home was just a short walk from the Oval Cricket Ground. Whenever the West Indies came to the UK to play England he would go and watch the match. I would sneak onto the ground with a friend and go round picking up discarded tickets from the floor. I thought it was a genius idea to stand outside and sell them to the people coming in. Had that happened today I would've been called a ticket tout, or worse.

I wouldn't call that my formal introduction into crime. I think I was just following my friend's lead with those cricket tickets; it wasn't a very lucrative venture and back then there were no mobile phones for distraction. However, you could call the first thing I stole that was my gateway into that world was a chocolate bar. I was fourteen years old. I'd nicked it from the local co-op. One bar became two, and two became ten. On one occasion I was caught by two policemen. The pair marched me to my door, the sight of which ignited a fury in my parents like no other. I received a traditional Jamaican belt-beating from my dad. The police officer decided to only caution me on this occasion but warned me that, if I kept on stealing, I would wind up in a lot of trouble.

But, I didn't stop, did I? I didn't have any role models around me. My dad certainly wasn't one. All the adults around me at the time were mostly drinkers or people with low aspirations. Growing up in the 70s, racism was everywhere. The National Front movement was rife. It was the time of the first racist murder of a black man in London: Kelso Cochrane. No one was ever convicted. Years later as a BBC journalist I made a documentary about it called 'Who Killed Kelso Cochrane'. Despite the inspirational men I saw on my TV, the truth is that they were few and far between. Today's Black Lives Matter movement has put many of the popular television shows I enjoyed watching in the 70s and 80s in the hot seat. Programmes like 'Love Thy Neighbour' and 'Mind Your Language' have been removed from today's broadcasting platforms for the racially stereotypical characters that they depicted. These programmes were indirectly the cause of many racial tensions. The mocking of black and other ethnic groups transferred from the television onto the streets. Kids like me were starting to be marginalised.

As you can expect, school then was not much help either. I started out at Crawford School which was fun. As I got older I moved to Archbishop Michael Ramsey school, a stone's throw from our front door. By then I was becoming more unruly which had started to get me into more and more trouble. On one occasion I was sent home with a message for my parents to come to school. One teacher had the nerve to look right in my mother's eye and call me a 'thing'. Now, my large round afro hair – I'll have you know it was quite stylish – often attracted attention. Being the son of a black father and a white mother, I rarely experienced any direct racism. There is no doubt that I was discriminated against, but there were very few times I could call it overt.

I witnessed outward racism inside my home more often than outside. When my mum and dad argued they would call each other every racist name under the sun: nigger, honky, black bastard, white whore – it became pretty normal to hear those terms in our house. In fact, it made hearing these insults outside of our four walls less offensive to me. All I did when other children called me a black bastard was wonder why they never called me a white one – I mean I am half white! But to have a teacher call me a 'thing'? My mum, there and then, slapped the teacher right across the face. She could be pretty feisty when necessary. It took a written apology from her to avoid criminal action and I still had to move school.

When teachers are calling young mixed-race teenagers like me 'things' what hope was there for me being guided through the right education? These incidents led to me becoming more anti-school and difficult. My parents' anger must have had a bearing on my own behaviour as I was also developing quite a reactionary temper. I remained in and out of trouble at my new school, William Penn in Red Post Hill, Dulwich. I began truanting from school almost right away. I started hanging about with what you would call the 'wrong sort of friends' as I was later told. They were mainly young black boys who also felt rejected by an education system that we felt had given up on us. It wasn't long before I had to change schools. Again.

At this time my cultural leanings also started to change. I found myself more accepted within black culture than I was within white. I was of mixed race and although I had never thought of myself as either black or white, I started to gravitate towards black culture and to hang out with more black guys in the neighbourhood. I have to admit that there were glimpses of another path for me. Despite my truanting, when I put in the effort at school, it was clear that I was bright and had capabilities. However, no one really saw this in me. Not even myself. I was good at the subjects that I paid attention to but concentration was difficult because my parents couldn't afford to give me the support I needed. I don't think they knew how. If they did I was oblivious to it as are most teenagers, distracted by our self-centered existence.

I quickly became a constant source of anxiety for my poor parents. This started a kind of cat-and-mouse game between my father and I. My dad's attempt to discipline me by keeping me indoors backfired horribly and led to me sneaking out. My parents would put me under a curfew to stop me from coming in late. If I wasn't home by a certain time, my dad would go to the lengths of locking the front door. My mother, however, would always relent and let me in. By then I had a ground floor bedroom with a window I could climb through. Upon realising this, my dad's tactic was to put up a strip of wood across it to stop me from sneaking out to party. Fat chance.

I fixed the strip of wood to make it easily removable. There was no way I'd be held back.

One night, there was a Shebeen, a drinking party, happening just down the road from our house. It was going to be one for the books. I waited till after midnight when my mother and my sisters were asleep, removed the wood and snuck out again. Turns out that night became memorable for a whole different reason. I walked in to see my father sitting there. My stomach dropped. I'm sure you can guess his reaction by now. He dragged me right back to my house. This was the first of many times this happened.

I was just trouble as a teenager. All I wanted was to be out with my friends, having fun, doing what they were doing. Nothing else mattered in my life. Back then I thought that my parents were being mean for stepping in my way. It even led me to run away from home on a couple of occasions. Now, I regret doing these selfish things. I feel guilt in the pit of my stomach for the stress and grief I caused them. I was walking right into the life they were trying to steer me away from.

By the time I was fifteen, my increasingly unruly behaviour was the reason for my exclusion from school. For me it was the age of disillusionment with education, with authority, with home, with everything. At school, I had grown to be a right little rebel. The things they were trying to teach me just didn't seem relevant to my life any more. In the end, I was dumped into Five Bridges School in Lambeth - a school for kids with similar behavioural problems. Why they thought this would be good for me I will never know. This was an Intermediate School which was supposed to provide me with opportunities to learn constructive patterns of behaviour. In fact, it was a den of thieves and misfits where there was no real control or direction. Eventually, I left.

In the late 70s and early 80s television advertising changed from promoting products to promoting lifestyles. Viewers like me were being sucked in to emulate the lifestyles and values of characters using the products on screen. Think the Cadbury's Flake Chocolate commercial or Levi Jeans for example. As a teenager, I was putty in their hands. I wanted what the other kids had, I wanted the coolest clothes and the latest trainers. I became heavily influenced by the change that I saw happening on television.

At that time, a few of my teenage mates had started to break into cars to steal expensive Blaupunkt and Pioneer car stereo systems and then sell them to a local garage. I started doing the same. It was easy and a quick way to make a buck. Smash the car window, reach through and grab. That was the technique. The biggest obstacle you would face was that sometimes the wires made it difficult to pull the stereo free.

I couldn't see any prospect of getting a job. That's mainly why I did this. Sure, I craved a certain lifestyle, but all I ever saw were the headlines of people like me, young coloured men, portrayed as young criminals. There is truth in that. But it was a direct consequence of being excluded from education and blocked from employment or from exploring our aspirations. It wasn't nice. Not much has changed today. I hate to use excuses for my actions but the reality of these issues is resurfacing as we can see from the Black Lives Matter movement. Everything seemed to be targeted against the particular community that I came from.

I embarked on the only path I saw that was offered to me. I started to smoke cannabis. I also got my first conviction for theft.

At about sixteen years old I graduated from breaking into cars to shoplifting and burglary, for which I received two convictions. My mates and I would take the stuff we'd stolen to the local pubs to sell onto customers. The landlords didn't mind and even bought what they fancied for themselves. Our introduction to the restaurant business presented an additional opportunity to earn a bit of money.

This involved doing the odd job for the Greek community that had started to emerge in Camberwell. One known family of criminals had opened a new restaurant and wanted to upset the competition in the area. They would pay me and my mates to go into rival cafés, pretend to have an argument amongst ourselves and start a fight. We'd throw the furniture around, smash up the crockery: the aim was to cause as much damage as possible. They'd pay £250 between five or six of us. We thought that was a good day's work. It didn't occur to me that this was another family's own business. All they were trying to do was earn an honest livelihood. I just did what I wanted, thinking that this was an easy way to make money. I had no thought of consequences.

Local youth clubs were supposed to be places of meaningful refuge from this lifestyle. Instead, most ended up being the very places that petty criminals gathered. It was at the St Giles Youth Club in Camberwell that I teamed up with Michael who was to become my best friend. He was a free spirit and had that happy-go-lucky attitude that I respected. At least that's what I thought at the time. He also lived his life with a sense of freedom that I lacked and craved. He was short and had a darker complexion than me. His medium build with brown copper coloured hair earned him the nickname 'Steelhead'. Michael remained my closest and best friend. I knew he had spent most of his life in a children's care home and in the care system. He was, as the kids say today, a 'roadman'; he was an individual that no-one messed with because he could fight. We did martial arts together in a local gym. He had an enthusiasm and dedication to the art that totally surpassed mine. He was small but fast, fit and ferocious. In all honesty, I was the same. Together we were feared, respected and always the focus of attention. He had such a strong influence on me because he was such a go-getter, and we were to share many experiences and adventures together, not all of them good. Just two years older than me I'd found a bit of a big brother in Michael.

Our reputation for having fun preceded us and was envied a lot by other guys. We had lively attitudes, dressed in the latest fashion and were streetwise. Many considered us to be bad boys. This attracted the girls but also made the boys square up; confrontations were inevitable.

The summer of 1985 was as carefree and fun as a summer could get. I was seventeen, wild, free and hustling in any way I could to make money. I remember meeting two girls who were very talented shoplifters. I'd never seen such skill! They were virtually professionals at what they did. For a while, we used to drive them around and keep an eye open for them as they 'worked'. Whatever they managed to steal, we would sell it on to the local shop owners and make good money.

One of these trips took us to Manchester where they 'cleaned out some designer shops' as we would say. With a car full of stolen gear, we turned round to head back to London. Michael got too tired to drive half way through. He asked me to take the wheel when we got to the motorway. What didn't occur to anyone as a problem was that not only did I not have a driving licence but that I did not know how to drive. Just another of our genius plans.

Michael explained what to do and how to put the car in gear. We were quickly driving in the outside lane at top speed. The only saving grace was that it was four in the morning and the road was quiet. I bombed it down the motorway, steering wheel held in a grip so tight my knuckles became white. The girl next to me was asleep. Michael and the other girl had fallen asleep in the back. I was literally on my own. As we edged towards London I realised that Michael had overlooked one minor point from his quickfire driving lesson: how to stop the car. I had to wake him up to tell me what to do. It was crazy and stupid, we were lucky not to have had an accident.

For better or for worse, this experience inspired me to buy my first car. Unlike many who, at that age, are helped by their parents to take their driving test, I just turned up one afternoon with a black Opel Commodore Coupe. As you do. The car itself wasn't new but it looked good. Though my mum was just happy to see her little boy, my dad still wasn't impressed. It was far too big a car for me but the desperation to own one and drive was far too strong to resist. That very same day I offered to give my sister Joanne a driving lesson. She had no driving licence and had never driven before which ultimately – surprise surprise – led to her driving head on into a tree crashing the car. Dad: 1. Raphael: 0.

That trip to the garage led to my first time in custody. I got into a serious dispute with the mechanic over the quality of the repair and the cost. He attacked me with a spanner so I fought back, wrestling him to the ground and hitting him on the head with the tool. Though he tried to take advantage of me and attacked me, I take full responsibility for my actions. I was sentenced to six months for Grievous Bodily Harm (GBH) in a young offenders prison which, after a month inside, was reduced to a probation and community order. That short stay in a young offenders institution was a real wake up call. It was a short sharp shock. Every morning at 6am music was piped into all the cells to wake us up. I had to make my bed and fold all of the items military style. It was regimented and the prison guards were threatening and menacing. So were the young offenders.

I had a fight on my first day during the exercise session, which was a football match. What I didn't know was the guy I ended up in a fight with was an amateur boxer. He caught me clean on the nose and put me on my arse. I got up and put him firmly on his arse. I felt no shame in reporting that I lost that fight.

Shortly after this I met another prisoner in the dining line. Now, when a young teen ends up inside it can have many different outcomes. This young white guy, thin, spotty with sad eyes that I'd met in the dining line told me that he was scared of some bullies. He said he was going to kill himself. I talked him down and reasoned with him that if he promised not to take his own life I would stand beside him every day to protect him from other prisoners. I knew I wouldn't really be able to protect him. I'd already lost the one fight I had. But I was genuinely shocked to hear what he said to me. That was the one good thing I can say came out of that situation.

It was my first experience of being locked up and it didn't phase me. In fact, it gave me more street-cred. When I came out, I was seen as being one of those guys who had been inside, and with that came a reputation. This experience should have been a springboard for change for me. It wasn't.

My time inside meant something very different to my parents. It was the final straw. At eighteen, I left home for good. I was now in a world of my own, refusing to listen to one word of my parents guidance or advice. After leaving home I teamed up with one of my friends who was renting a flat in a notoriously rough estate in Peckham. We didn't have any furniture so the only reasonable thing to do in our minds was to break into a furniture warehouse to steal some. We kitted-out the flat and it looked really nice but the high was short lived. We'd been spotted moving furniture into the property so it wasn't long before the police arrested us. Again, I'd acted without consideration. This self-serving act of desperation earned me another community service.

It still didn't stop me. Even during my community service I broke into a few other warehouses. It'd steal whatever I could sell to make money. I'd almost seen out my community service order when I was stopped by the police and found to be in possession of some cannabis. Stop and search was not new to me and many of my black mates were regularly targeted by the police. Sometimes it was justified but most of the time it was just because we were teenagers who looked like we were up to no good. As a result, my punishment was extended to two hundred hours of community service and a longer probation order. At the time, I was sleeping with a girl from Brixton who had her own flat. I ended up spending a lot of time crashing at hers to escape my own reality. With no one to guide me back to a law-abiding life, no one to show me a different way, I inevitably went back to the only life I knew.

Many of my friends had started to carry knives so I did as well. I carried a Rambo style knife in a holster strapped around my chest to make a statement. I carried it to protect myself and make others fear me because that's what you had to do on the streets. All the street kids knew this. Carrying a knife is wrong. There's no question about that. It is an attacking weapon, not a defensive weapon, so to use the excuse that it is for protection is wrong. Carrying a knife led to two events that I will never forget.

The first thing it led to was me getting kidnapped and beaten by the older brother and friends of a former friend I had stabbed for being a grass. I can remember my friends and I were fighting with this person and his people. In the mayhem, I was on my back being hit in the face, when I pulled the knife out and poked it into the buttocks of the guy hitting me. It wasn't that deep but it was enough for him to know I was serious. It was a scary moment for both of us and he climbed off me and ran. I thought that was the end of it.

Late one evening a few days later I was walking home. Two men pounced on me and bundled me into the back of a car. I was taken to a park, stripped naked, badly beaten and left in a ditch. I made my way to the roadside totally naked and begged a passer-by to give me their jumper to use as a makeshift skirt to cover me from the waist down. I made my way back to my flat, seriously shaken up by the whole experience.

The second incident led to me being stabbed and my cheek sliced open. I was lucky to survive that attack. It happened when I was leaving the flat of the girl I was seeing in Brixton. Three young guys jumped me on the stairway as I was making my way to my car. They intended to rob me but I put up as much of a fight as I could. I landed some punches on one of the robbers, cutting his eye and mouth. He pulled out a knife – I didn't have mine as I didn't carry it all the time – and he stabbed me hard in the side of my head just a fraction away from my temple. I was then overpowered by the other two and pinned to the ground and given a good beating. The one whose lip I busted then pushed the blade to the side of my face and ran it down my cheek, slicing it open. They ran off and left me there to bleed. I held my face together, got in my car and drove to my flat.

When I arrived Michael was there. He took me straight to the hospital. He called my mum who burst in followed by my sisters Belinda, Hazel and Joanne. I can't imagine what it was like for my mum at the time, but as I tell you this I can feel that gut wrenching sorrow of pain I would have felt as a parent. I did not tell the hospital staff or the police who attended what happened. I just let them stitch my face then left the hospital.

There was a lot of talk of revenge for what I suffered. There was a rage among my friends and a frustration that there was no-one to blame who could be held responsible. The attack and stabbing made it clear that I was not the invincible kid I thought I was. The scar that runs down the slide of my face serves as a constant reminder of the street life that inevitably ends in prison or death.

Looking back at those days, I was caught up in a culture that was violent and dangerous. It was all around me and couldn't be avoided. It is easy to say you could walk away, but where could I go? At the time, I did not give a thought to the consequences of my actions and neither did the people around me. Most teenagers don't. Of course, today, as an adult, I have completely different values and I understand the difference between good and bad. Truth and honesty matter now more than anything. I know that profoundly, because of all that has happened to me since. By now I've met many good people with fine morals, whereas as a kid back then, I had no positive role-models and no mentors. There were no alternative lifestyles and there was no-one reaching out to offer one. I don't claim that it was other people's responsibility to save me. I'm just stating a fact that if there was anyone or anything that could have changed my direction in life it wasn't something I was aware of. Any resources that were available were out of reach for kids like me. There were no mobile phones or internet in the 80's. We all had to find our own way in life and this didn't always work out for the best.

By now, Michael and I had moved to somewhere known as the White House. The White House was a bit of a rabbit warren spread over four floors. The main entrance was on the side of the building. As you entered and climbed the stairs there were doors everywhere. It was occupied mostly by young men but I remember there were also a couple of women staying there as well. It was a lively place, shall we call it that? Most of the tenants staying there were on probation and had come into contact with the police or the criminal justice system in some way. Some had been referred there as a sort of halfway house as part of their probation.

The flow of people coming and going was endless and the stolen property came and went. There were clothes, VHS video players, and jewellery. It began to pile up around us. Some of it we stole ourselves and some of it we bought from others and sold at a profit. We always had a large stash of personal weed and hash to smoke and even tried becoming drug dealers on a small scale, but it just wasn't our thing so we stopped.

At first, we shared a large room at the front of the house. After a six-month stint in Michael's room I got to know the landlord, John, and persuaded him to let me have a room of my own. Even better, I managed to get the council to pay my rent.

John lived on the ground floor with a fitted basement that was one of the better parts of the property. He had a room decked out as a full disco and also a swimming pool in the garden. There was always something happening or a party taking place. He was a shifty character and I'm convinced he was an old school villain and a feeder of information to the police; I am sure he was into a lot more than I ever knew. He was always happy to take in people irrespective of what they had been up to. He must have been in his 50s at the time. I remember he drove this big silver Mercedes which was always parked on the drive by the main entrance. A big contrast to my little Black MG Midget and Michael's Fiat X19 parked on the kerb alongside.

I got along very well with John. He gave me the responsibility of keeping an eye out for him and of making sure everyone behaved themselves. It was a bit like being a prefect at school – an experience I can assure you I was not familiar with! There were always shifty characters around and people would be coming and going all the time. There were always girls about, usually between 18 and 25 and from every background. Not everybody knew each other but we would all be respectful when we passed each other in the corridors. It really was a bit of a commune.

The White House wasn't a house where drugs were sold but in those days I think most residents smoked cannabis. Some guys might have been taking something stronger but we all kept ourselves to ourselves and never asked questions. It was an unspoken rule and it was all about trust. That is the way that criminal minds work.

At that time I was free. I had no responsibilities. I wasn't paying any bills. I didn't have a care in the world. At night, I go clubbing with Mike and friends in the West End, or East End, South London, out West, it didn't matter, I'd go anywhere.

I would just go out and enjoy myself.

46

I was the sort of person that when I turned up at a club, or party, wherever the most fun was, I'd be there. If there was fiery dancing, I'd be in that corner and I'd have an amazing time. I'd have one night stands. Sometimes they'll be trouble at these clubs with guys from other areas who didn't like the kind of bounce that we had in our step and got offended. And that could sometimes explode into some real violent fights. Not many but there were a couple I really didn't have any qualms or even a conscience about. To be honest, I didn't have anything to have a conscience about at that time.

"SHE'D FILL MY EARS WITH ALL HER ASPIRATIONS. SHE WANTED TO GO TO UNIVERSITY. SHE WAS DETERMINED TO DO SOMETHING BETTER WITH HER LIFE. DEEP DOWN INSIDE OF ME, I THINK I WANTED SOMETHING LIKE THAT TOO."

02

A SOUTH LONDON BOY

CHAPTER 2

A South London Boy

The summer of 1988 heralded a different era. Fashion had changed. Funnily enough, the kids today wear almost the same things as we did back then. Ripped jeans, designer labels and fashionable t-shirts made up our new uniform. Dreadlocks (or dreads as we used to call them) had become both a fashion statement and a movement amongst us rebellious boys and girls, and both white and black kids were a part of that statement. The country had just stepped out of the National Front era and Margaret Thatcher found other ways to make herself busy. She introduced draconian laws and expanded the new Crown Prosecution Service to counterbalance increased police powers. These culminated in riots across the country as poor communities – especially those populated by young black men – protested the disproportionate use of 'stop and search' ('sus') powers against them. My friends and I were oblivious to it all, but would be targeted as a result.

Michael and I were well settled into our flat in the White House by then. I would spend hours cleaning and polishing my car in the summer sun. It would sit parked beside Michael's car: a blue convertible Fiat. Music would blare and girls would stare and coo from the other side of the road. We were two teenage men without a care in the world and very much a product of our times. Despite what we thought of ourselves, we were the 'bad kids' pimped out by politicians as examples to justify new laws and legislations that were being introduced. As far as the world was concerned we were a pair of young, black, unemployed men with criminal convictions. As you know, we were involved in crime. By now our antics had evolved to follow the path of the slightly older criminals around us. They would adopt a more careful approach, solely motivated by not getting caught. They were the ones to look up to and that's all they wanted, so that's all I wanted. Neither Michael nor I ever had the desire to look for work or to earn legitimate money. We had a lifestyle that was working out just fine. But those summer months brought about a whole new change in my life. For one, 1988 was the summer that I met Nancy.

Living in the same flat meant that Michael and I had come to do everything together, including chat up girls. The only time we parted ways was when one of us had a girl coming back. We'd formed a little agreement. If I was bringing a girl back, Michael would leave. If he brought a girl back, I would leave. It was as simple as that. Quite the pair of gentlemen, don't you think? On one occasion that summer, Michael had double-booked himself. We both had a lot of girlfriends back in those days. So much so that we had developed a contingency plan for this exact scenario. When Michael was double booked, I would take his car keys and his car. That way, if one of the girls came round the corner, she would see that his car wasn't there and assume that he was out. This particular time it was Nancy. I had no idea who she was but she caught me as she turned round the corner. When I told her that Michael wasn't there and she seemed disappointed, I offered to take her out. We hopped into the car and drove off to my friend's flat in Camberwell. We smoked a little weed, kissed and smooched but nothing major.

We talked and we laughed, and it surprised me to see how well we got on. I offered to drop her home to Beckenham which was only around the corner from where I lived. We parked the car about two roads from where she was living to avoid her parents seeing. Just as I was about to pull out a woman and man jumped out in front of the car screaming at the top of their lungs. I sprang out of the car. It was Nancy's mum and step-dad. They yelled at me for keeping their daughter out past midnight. I must have then said something cheeky – knowing me, I probably did – because Nancy's mum slapped me clean across the face. I was in shock. Not that it should even need saying, but I have never been the type of man that puts his hand on a woman. I just stood still until auto-pilot kicked in and I drove back home to my flat. When I came home I saw Michael sitting alone. I asked him what happened to the girl that he was meant to meet.

"She didn't show," he said. The whole time I thought I was doing him a favour. What I didn't realise was that he had meant to meet Nancy.

My relationship with Nancy started a couple of days later when her mum invited me to come over one evening. That smack must have been playing on her mind, churning her tummy with a guilt that could only be put to rest with an awkward dinner. Think about it, I was this cocky, cheeky twenty year old who grew up on a council estate. My world revolved around council flats, rampant unemployment and crime. Barely anyone I knew had achieved very much at school and each day we earned just enough to loosen the choke-hold that money, or lack thereof, had on our lives. The minute I entered their house my demeanour changed. I had stepped into a universe of semi-detached and terraced homes that people actually owned. It was worlds away from my own experience.

During that dinner, Nancy's mum lectured me about how I was too old for her sixteen year old daughter. That age gap never did stop us. It could, however, make things awkward. Nancy used to go to school down the road from where I lived. I'd pull up outside in my convertible MG to the sound of school bells and jealous whispers of other girls desperate to be the one jumping into my front seat. Nancy was Head Girl and she was getting into my car. She was smart. She was learning French, German and Russian at the same time. She travelled. She had a style and swagger that set her apart from all the other girls I was sleeping with. I really did get around back then. I was having sex everyday with different girls who in turn were having sex with different guys. Life back then was a haze of smoke, music and good times. I won't deny the bad-boy image that I had. It was the type of image that attracted those girls to me in the first place. They all loved the idea of being the bad-boy's girlfriend.

Nancy never knew about any of the other girls. However, the other girls knew about her. Another girl, Kate, who I was regularly sleeping with at the time started to become jealous of Nancy and I, so much so that she wrote me a love letter. She said it all on the page. She told me how upset I was making her and that she wished I would ditch Nancy and just be with her instead. Of course I didn't, and her resentment began to fester. There's every chance that this jealousy drove the lies she told about me later.

Nancy wasn't like those other girls to me. She was still somebody after we had sex. With anyone else, I'd be up and out before I could zip my fly, but with her I would just lay there and listen. She'd fill my ears with all her aspirations. She wanted to go to university. She was determined to do something better with her life. Deep down inside of me, I think I wanted something like that too. Nancy was one of the few people around me who had a purpose. I needed something like that. That's one of the reasons I was so attracted to her. Maybe Nancy had been like the others and been seduced by my bad-boy lifestyle. The truth is that she also saw a sensitive side to me. A better side. For all the differences we had, there was just something deeper that pulled us together. Nancy instinctively knew that I was in desperate need of better guidance. She was one of the few people around me who saw that I could do better, even though I thought I lived the best life anyone could ask for.

I was still heavily involved in crime at this point but my business and personal life were oil and water for me. I would never involve Nancy, or any or the other girls, in what I was doing. I'm sure they could've guessed that I was up to some very illegal stuff but I would never tell them. I had a car and my own place; the only thing I didn't have was a regular, honest income.

By this time, Michael and I had started to do things separately. After a bit of a fallout I moved out of the big front room we shared in the White House into the flat just above it. We were still tight and fiercely loyal to each other, but I started to make new friends. I began hanging out with these guys who would snort and freebase cocaine. I dabbled. For me it was all about experimenting. We'd hit up the nightclubs in the West End and strut around like we owned the place. There was never any trouble; it was all about a good time. I loved to dance and would let the whole atmosphere sweep me up in a cloud of cocaine, bass and dancing bodies. Michael was never into that scene and his disinterest ended up putting a strain on our friendship.

Another new friend I made was Jona. He's what you could call another dodgy resident of the White House. White-skinned with Asian features, he moved in after being referred by the probation office. When he came over we'd watch a video or smoke drugs. Sometimes we would just talk. Jona felt rejected by his family and my door was one of the few that was always open to him. Compared to Michael and Jona, my upbringing had been fairly stable. I didn't know what it was like to be separated from your parents and having to fend for yourself from a young age. I had no way of knowing just how hard it was to have to bounce in and out of care homes, jostled between different foster parents. Michael and Jona were my only insight into that experience and I remember being struck by how unfair society is, often to those who need its help the most.

Of course, there was a business element to Jona's and my relationship. He was a thief, and a good one at that. Whenever he had something to sell, he'd come to me first then I'd find a buyer and get a little slice of the pie. That said, I hadn't lost my light fingers. One summer's day I'd gone out shoplifting with my mates. We set out to 'pick up' items that people had ordered from us in a local shopping centre. Our plan was simple. We would take our special shoplifting bags which had to be big, branded from a different shopping centre and couldn't by any means be see-through. What you'd do was put something in the bottom of the bag to make it wide enough to keep the top gaping open. We'd buy one or two items, but the others we'd slip into the bag as we traipsed around the store. A security guard must have been watching us from the beginning because as soon as we left the shop he pounced. I managed to alert my friend who fled from the scene but it meant that I got caught.

The coppers decided not to arrest me this time, but they did escort me from the station back to my flat on Lawrie Park Road. Under my bed they found a collection of clothes still in their wrappers with the labels still on. They asked me if the stuff belonged to me. Calm as ever I declared that I'd bought it from someone. Put off by the hassle of proving I was lying, they charged me with attempted shoplifting and my probation period was extended. That was my eighth conviction.

After that, things had to change and I knew it. I earned very little money from being a supervisor for John and the cash I made from crime wasn't anything to sing home about. At this time Nancy and I had started spending more time together. We'd waste days just lounging in the park, and long summer nights loving under the pitch black sky. Inspired by my chats with her and this change in me, I was persuaded by my probation officer to enrol on a college course in journalism in Lewisham. For a split second it looked as if the dust might finally settle. However, something unexpected bundled in that shook my life up again.

I knew Claudia from when we were kids on the Crawford Estate. Now we were all grown up she'd moved into the same block of flats as a mate of mine. One night, when I was at his place, she showed up. As the night drifted on we found our way into her mother's flat just below and we made love.

She fell pregnant and in October 1988, she gave birth to my son. It was a difficult time. We weren't in a relationship and in my mind she was trapping me. She'd plotted to have my kid to pull me away from the other girls and the life I was living. That's what I thought. In truth, I was a deviant bad-boy on the street, sleeping with lots of different girls. Claudia getting pregnant wasn't fair on either of us, but most of all it wasn't fair on our child. The relationship between Claudia and I was practically non-existent. I wasn't there when Claudia gave birth. I did turn up at the hospital the following day and I remember holding my son amazed that I had become a dad. I was twenty years old.

I had a son but I wasn't a father. I was a useless dad. I had no idea what to do, no guidance from my own father, no other man that I could talk to about this new responsibility. When Claudia and the baby left the hospital, although I showered them both with gifts, I didn't really want to have anything to do with her. Maybe I wasn't capable of having a proper relationship. There's every chance I was too immature and I was certainly too unreliable. But that decision remains one of my biggest regrets. Why didn't I see the situation for what it was? I paid the price for that choice by not being allowed to see my son and it's a pain that has gnawed deep inside of me for more than thirty years.

I have not in all these years had a conversation with my son. He has grown up, become a man and never spoken to me; his biological dad. It chokes me up to even talk about it. My absence in his life fills me with a sadness that nothing could ease. During prison I kept a diary. I would put all my thoughts about him into those pages. My hope was that on the day of my release, if I was unable to find the words to express my loss and love that these words would at least go in some way to show that I had not abandoned him. But I have not been able to show him these yet.

So this is who I was: a mixed-race boy from a law-abiding family who'd got a girl pregnant and socialised with petty criminals. I told you I was no angel. But, despite my past involvement in a few violent acts, I was not the monster I was about to be portrayed as.

A SUSPECTED MURDERER

"YOU ARE POWERLESS IN THE FACE OF EVERYTHING THAT IS HAPPENING TO YOU, AND HAVE NO IDEA AS TO WHAT MIGHT HAPPEN NEXT."

CHAPTER 3

A suspected murderer

I t was the 19th of December 1988 and I was at home in my flat. Loud and sudden noises broke my sleep. At first, I thought it was Michael and his brother Lloyd fighting. Lloyd had come round the night before and crashed in the bottom space of my flat. I'd never really seen him and Michael get physical before but they argued often enough to make it plausible. Reluctantly, I lifted myself up and sitting on the edge of my bed, I lit a cigarette.

I was annoyed to have been disturbed at such an early hour in the morning. I shrugged on a T-shirt, a pair of boxers and shuffled down the stairs to see what all the fuss was about. What I saw shocked me fully awake. Lloyd was walking towards the front door with his hands in the air. I came down a few of the steps to see men dressed in dark clothes. Even though their masks covered their faces, they had a menacing look about them. They clocked my presence and in an instant, they pointed their guns in my direction.

"POLICE! POLICE! PUT YOUR HANDS IN THE AIR OR I'LL SHOOT."

I had no idea at the time, but I later learned that this was the S19 special armed response unit of the MET police. I can't remember what weapons they were holding but they had handguns and something bigger that looked like a machine gun. My hands hung in the air and my whole body trembled. The cigarette was still in my mouth and it was burning closer to my lips. I kept shaking my head. The cigarette smoke started to burn my eyes and I went to bring my hand to my mouth to drop it. All hell broke loose. One of the masked men dropped to his knees and aimed his gun to fire at me. An officer must have told him not to shoot because instead, the masked man screamed at me to put my hands back in the air. I did. As dramatic as I knew this was, it still scared me senseless. That had to be their tactic; to scare me. I couldn't pose a threat. I was still in my T-shirt and boxers, so it was obvious I couldn't have been concealing a weapon or anything else. Well, it worked. I'd been involved in crime and violence, that you know. But having a gun pointed at me, was a whole other level.

My mouth was dry. The cigarette was burning my lips, so I just let it fall. The shouting and the noise consumed the air, disorienting me physically as well as mentally. The men told me to turn around and walk back towards them. As I came closer they swarmed all over me. My hands were cuffed in some kind of plastic tie that dug into the skin of my wrists.

"IS THERE ANYONE ELSE IN THE FLAT?"

It was all happening so fast. The last thing I remember was being spun around and taken out of the room. I remember the glimmer of the cigarette stub burning into the carpet. The police made a ragdoll out of me. They dragged me by the arms. I had no shoes on and they were pulling me faster than I could walk, scraping the soles of my feet.

My legs gave way and they shoved me down the stairs backwards, and every step punched a different part of my back.

I caught a glimpse of Jona. Two policemen pinned him down to the floor and knelt on his body. They held guns to his head which made his eyes bulge out in terror. The whole scene was shocking.

As they dragged me out of the building's front door, I found myself amazed at how many armed police lined the path outside. Some were uniformed and some were in plain-clothes.

This was a huge operation. Police cars and vans pierced the air with their flashing blue lights. It almost looked like a film set. I could not figure out how I'd become the star of the show. I'd not done anything so serious as to deserve this. One of the officers in uniform approached me. He told me that he was arresting me for aggravated burglary. I remember asking him what aggravated burglary meant.

"Breaking into other people's homes with weapons." Before I could ask anything else, I was dragged away and thrown in the back of a police van. Michael and Lloyd were already sitting there. A moment later someone opened the van door and we were asked to state our names. They took Michael and Lloyd out of the van. I was positioned between two plain-clothes officers, after which the doors were slammed shut. Sirens blazed as the convoy of vans took off at high speed. It was surreal.

As I started to get my breath back a sense of fear engulfed me. I find it difficult even now, to put into words. The second I saw guns pointed at me, I knew this was something serious. Aggravated burglary surely didn't warrant guns. Or did it? I didn't know. The thoughts ricocheted through my mind, which was almost paralysed by the terror of the situation.

I stood petrified in front of a custody officer who asked me my name and a few other questions. My body still shook from the ordeal of my arrest. I told him my name, date of birth, address and whether I was employed. He informed me that I was being arrested and cautioned on suspicion of aggravated burglary.

He asked me if I understood the charge. I said yes. He asked if I wanted a solicitor. I said yes, if I needed one. I didn't know. The custody officer listed all the property that I had on me, which was essentially my T-shirt and boxer shorts. I was led into a cell and left alone. It stank of urine. The wall had a window made of very thick glass at the top of it and a wooden bench fixed towards the bottom, which was topped with a blue plastic mattress. Names and abusive words scattered the walls, door and wooden bench, etched in by those who had previously occupied this cell. I sat with my head in my hands, not knowing whether to cry or scream.

Outside the cell, I could hear noises and muffled conversations. I put my ear to the cell door to try and hear better but it was too thick. I sat on the plastic mattress for what seemed like an eternity, trying to keep a grip on my sanity until, finally, the cell door opened.

A short stocky man in a blue pinstripe suit announced himself as the duty solicitor. He had been contacted by the police as this was the procedure, and he told me that he was there to help me. I asked him what was happening. He told me that I had been arrested on a number of serious offences, but he didn't know any of the details at that moment. He offered to represent me and, not knowing any better at the time, I accepted. Within minutes of giving me this crushing information he left me, and I was abandoned to suffer in my ignorance.

I couldn't tell you how long I was left in isolation. In a cell, you lose all track of time. Eventually, the door opened again and I was led into a room by the very same pair of plain-clothes officers who had bundled me in the back of the police van. I was instructed to take off my shorts and T-shirt and put on a white jumpsuit. They put my clothes into separate bags. I think it was at this point that they also took DNA samples from me.

As I changed, the custody officer said he wanted to take my photo. I asked why. He said that I was going to be transferred to Reigate Police Station in Surrey, and that the photo was to prove I'd not been beaten up whilst at Croydon. I thought it strange that one police station had to prove to another that they hadn't assaulted me. But this was 1988. Things were different then. The Special Patrol Group – a.k.a. the SPG – were a Metropolitan Police unit that had been disbanded in 1987. They were responsible for the death of the anti-Nazi protester Blair Peach, who had become a household name. They were a unit that local communities in London feared, as they patrolled with baseball bats and were known to assault the suspects they arrested in the back of their vans. There was a lot less accountability back then. So, I signed the piece of paper permitting them to take my photograph. On that piece of paper, I remember writing down that this was the reason the officer told me that he wanted the photograph. I was then escorted back to my cell.

It was a few hours before the cell door opened again, and through the small, dirty window high up on the wall, I could see that it had gone from light to dark outside. I was then ushered out, and told to line up with all the other guys that had been arrested at the White House earlier that day, ready for the transfer to Reigate. One of the same plain-clothes police officers that had been interacting with me throughout the day, handcuffed me, and another stood close by. They wanted to put a bag over my head as they took us out to the van. I was convinced it was a trick to beat me up, so I told them to fuck off. They forced it over my head anyway. Believe it or not, when you're in handcuffs, there is not a lot you can do. As we went outside, I quickly understood the reason for covering my face. Crowds of journalists with cameras and flashguns swarmed over the scene, all eager to snap a picture of me. Little did I know, I was about to be front-page news for days.

The flash of the lights stunned me through the holes in the bag, and I was frog marched to the car that was waiting for me. The convoy then set off with motorbike outriders, with sirens screaming, and a helicopter whirring overhead. Yet another bizarre, and terrifying ordeal. You have no idea what it's like until you've experienced it. You become powerless in the face of everything that is happening to you, and have no idea as to what might happen next.

We arrived at Reigate. It was as if the circus was coming to town. Once again, I went through the same procedure with their custody sergeant asking me to repeat my name etc. Once they'd completed their paperwork they locked me in my cell.

By now I was angry, as well as afraid. As a young 20-year-old, I wasn't renowned for my patience at the best of times, and had very little control over my temper. All of this was just too much. I was probably quite abusive towards the police officers. At that point, I still didn't know what was going on. Nothing I'd done could explain this kind of attention and this type of behaviour from the police. The fact is that I was in serious trouble, but still didn't know why, and it was driving me crazy. The fear still sat beneath my anger. All of us that had been arrested, would put on this act of bravado; we would refuse to show any weakness but we were all equally scared.

It was still the 19th of December, and late that evening I was taken for an interview for the very first time. Once again, I was taken by the same two plainclothes police officers. As I was moved from my cell to the interview room, there was the sound of a dog continuously barking outside in the courtyard. It served as another reminder of the security we were under. I wondered if they thought they had actually arrested some really bad criminals when really it was just us normal kids. The interview room was small. It had a little table. It was here that I learned the names of these two plain-clothes detectives; Detective Constable David Manhire and Detective Constable James Gallagher, who sat opposite me with a notebook.

Gallagher was the older man. He must have been in his

50s, given his tweed suit and the pipe he was smoking. As he peered at me over his glasses, he reminded me a bit of Sherlock Holmes. His colleague, DC David Manhire, was younger, with a stocky build and wore casual dress. He had an attitude of permanent contempt. It was obvious that he just didn't like me.

I'll admit that I had a bit of an attitude myself. Mine was more of a jumpy, fearful kind of nervousness, whereas his attitude was more complacent backed by the power of authority. The dynamic in that room was not healthy from the very beginning. New guidelines requiring police to tape-record interviews to protect suspects, under the Police and Criminal Evidence Act, had recently come into force. The pair put a fresh audio cassette into the tape machine and started by announcing the day, time and who was present. That was the two detectives, the duty solicitor Jeremy Bull and me.

Then the questions started.

"When did you crash the Spitfire? Why did you kick him to death?" I was dumbfounded. What on earth were they talking about? What Spitfire? Who was I supposed to have kicked to death? This was just crazy, scary and stupid. I was trying to guess what was going on from clues in their questions. These officers threw things at me verbally, that I could not believe. Kick a man to death? They had my heart pounding. I was confused, and uncomfortable. I answered all the questions that I could, but it just meant repeating myself. I don't know. I did not. It wasn't me! Not I.

They kept telling me that people were saying things about me, which were very obviously not true. If people were implicating me in the kicking of a man to death, then these could only be downright lies. I wasn't involved in anything like that. Having allowed this line of questioning to go on for some time, my solicitor eventually advised me not to say anymore.

Despite everything I said, and my complete denials, I could tell that DC Manhire was still convinced that I was guilty. I was his target, and nothing else mattered. All the words in the world wouldn't have made a difference to him, he'd have just dismissed it. I would describe him as a man in a hurry. He just wanted to get it done and dusted. I got the impression he had been told to get a confession out of me at all costs. It was almost Christmas, I think I was standing between him going home to his family. I had to disappoint him. The other detective, DC Gallaher was more pensive, and didn't seem to have the same pressing agenda. Now and then he would stop, and draw on his pipe, and think. I don't think he was at all convinced by his colleague's conviction of my guilt, but for now, he kept his thoughts to himself.

I was really worried after that first interview. I was worried about the things they were both asking about and telling me. But there was a little bit of me that felt relieved, because I knew whatever they were interrogating me about, I had no involvement in. When they took me back to my cell, it was in the early hours of the morning. The dog was still barking. I couldn't sleep. They didn't leave it long before they disturbed me again. It wouldn't do for me to be rested. They took me back into the interview room, which stank of Gallagher's pipe, and they continued with the same kind of unanswerable questions as earlier, none of which made any sense. I became the same broken record I'd been the day before. I don't know. It wasn't me. No, not me.

It was now the following day, the 20th of December. I had no idea what was going on on the outside. I didn't see the headlines, and the photos in the papers, until much later. I had no idea about the effect that they were having on my parents and family. There was a sinister picture of my eye, peering through a hole in the hood they had put over my head, as they transferred me to Reigate Police Station. Headlines like "Killing for Kicks" were slapped on the front page of the Daily Mail. There were eyewitness reports from passers-by who watched the arrest take place. Apparently, I was public enemy number one.

It was reported that a team of forty-five officers were involved in the dawn raid. There were marksmen in blue berets, and armed officers disguised as milkmen, dustmen and builders who had kept watch on the house in advance. We were being described as the 'M25 Gang.' A total of twelve people had been arrested that day.

A builder working opposite the White House, said it all ended in minutes. Eleven people were brought out in handcuffs, seven black men and four white. No shots were fired. The suspects were put in police vans, the black men separate from the others. Now, why on earth should that be? If that isn't enough of a clear indication of racism, then I don't know what is. This was the 80s, the UK was riddled with racism. A Mrs Barbara Hamilton was walking her Alsatian dog as the police carried out the raid. She said the police already had one man with dreadlocks sitting in the back of a van before she saw another handcuffed Rastafarian being brought out.

Well, it's obvious, isn't it? The second man Barbara Hamilton saw, was me, because the first would have been Michael. I'd started growing dreadlocks when I was eighteen, mainly as a fashion statement rather than a religious symbol. Michael and I were the only two arrested who sported dreadlocks.

These were the stories and the headlines printed on the morning of my arrest, and were exactly what my parents, friends, family, strangers, people all over this country would have been reading. I bet half of them probably breathed a sigh of relief when the terrible M25 gang had been captured, just in time for Christmas. At the time, I knew nothing of this.

I was back with Manhire and Gallagher, who were telling me that my girlfriend had made a statement to police. I asked, "Who's that?" They told me it was a girl called Kate, who had told them I had given her items of jewellery. They started to ask me about jewellery and balaclavas. What jewellery? I had no idea what they were talking about.

"Are all your girlfriends white?" asked Manhire. "Don't you like black girls?"

What sort of random questions were these? More to the oint was what did they have to do with what they were accusing me of? I didn't understand. As it happens, most of the girls that I was sleeping with around that time were white, but I was also sleeping with black girls. What difference does that make? It certainly seemed to make a hell of a lot of difference to the police, in the way that they were interrogating me.

After two days of these interrogations, my head was spinning. I was confused. I was mad. On the third day, the police loaded me into a van and took me to another police station in Caterham. They said they were ready to charge me, and then left me alone for hours. I was terrified. I was scared. I didn't really believe they were going to charge me. How could they? I had done nothing. It was like torture, not knowing what was going to happen next. Time dragged along, and the cell door opened. A sergeant I had not met before took me out. He read from a sheet of paper that I was being charged with murder, robbery and wounding.

By now, I'd long lost the ability to even hear what he was saying. Who had been murdered? It's all I was thinking. Who were they talking about? I had absolutely no idea. Afterwards I was just put back into a cell, and left to stew in my fear.

Much later, DC Manhire and DC Gallagher came back to the cell for formal mugshots and fingerprints. My fingers were pressed into ink and pressed onto paper, the officers rolling each finger so hard, I thought they were trying to break them. They were gloating about the fact that I'd been charged. It was now the 22nd of December. They told me that I was the only one, out of the twelve arrested, who had been charged. Now they could go home and enjoy their Christmas. I will never forget the words of DC Manhire as he left.

"I hope you roast in Hell!" he said, locking the door behind him.

I don't think his tone indicated righteous indignation on behalf of the victims of the crimes, but a kind of indifferent satisfaction. I don't think he cared whether I was guilty or not guilty. It was just, "We've got the charge. Job done!"

For me, this was the deep realisation that the life I had been enjoying up until that moment, was over. "Roast in hell!" meant no more driving my sports car; no more nights in the clubs, with the girls; no more playing tennis with my friends; no more wheeling and dealing. No, the life that I knew, had come to a crashing halt, and I was devastated. What I didn't know then was that this was going to continue for a very, very long time.

I was in the police station for three days in total. In those three days, I probably only slept for a couple of hours. This was a deliberate tactic on their part. They would have dogs outside barking. They would have officers come to my cell door, open the hatch every now and again, and slam it to wake me up. Then there would be a 'friendly officer' who would poke his head round the cell door and ask me if there is anything I wanted to get off my chest.

I didn't know it then, but there were lots of strange things going on in that police station at the time. The one thing that sticks in my mind, is the tactics used by the two police officers who arrested me.

They played the good cop, bad cop routine. The good cop was DC Gallaher, smoking his pipe, and staying mainly in the background. The bad cop was, without a doubt, DC Manhire, with his sleeves rolled up, leaning on the table. I think he'd seen too many television programmes. He made it obvious that he thought I was some horrible animal who'd committed these horrible crimes.

All the information he had could point to the fact that I was guilty. It was his job to make me confirm it.

Although I had been advised by the solicitor to say "no comment" to all of the questions, as far as I was concerned, I had nothing to hide. I had not been involved with the crimes they were accusing me of. There could not be any witnesses, because I had not been there. No one could have seen me. So I was cheeky with my responses. In the moments when they entertained the possibility that I was elsewhere at the time of the murder, they couldn't understand why I didn't remember things that had only happened a few days before. The reason was, of course, because I lived an erratic weed-fuelled daze of a life, and had no reason to remember my day to day existence. I had no routine or expectation. Nevertheless, I tried hard to give them as much detail as I could about who I was with, what I did and where I was during the times they were saying I was involved in these crimes. Needless to say they would not believe me. They knew better. After three days of fruitless questioning had made no difference, they had done their job. I was to be taken in a prison van to Brixton Prison, an old Victorian jail in south-east London. It was the 23rd of December.

Up to this point, I still hadn't seen any of my family, or spoken to anybody other than my solicitor. I felt completely alone. Hearing that I was going to be sent to Brixton prison scared me to my core. Brixton was a very different place to the youth prisons I had been sent to in the past.

I was just twenty, and I was being placed in an adult prison. It was a maximum-security establishment, with a reputation for being one of the harshest out there. Inside sat a special remand unit for Category A prisoners: the prison within a prison. The very thought of it terrified me.

"I WENT THROUGH THE NOW-FAMILIAR PROCESS OF BEING ASKED MY NAME AND FOR ALL MY DETAILS. I WAS TOLD FROM THIS MOMENT ON, I WOULD BE PRISONER ROWE MP3660. MY IDENTITY WAS REDUCED TO A NUMBER."

PRISONER
MP3660 ROWE

04

CHAPTER FOUR

Prisoner MP 3660 Rowe

I was escorted to the prison van and taken to Brixton Prison. No helicopter and outriders this time. Michael was also being shipped to Brixton Prison, in a separate van, having been charged with the same offences as me. Upon arrival, the police handed us over to the prison staff. They treated us like pieces of meat. I was thrust into a cubicle and shouted at by officers. They forced me to take off my white overalls and put on their prison clothes. Black shoes, brown T-shirt and brown trousers. Not one of them fitted me.

I went through the now-familiar process of being asked my name and all my details. I was told from this moment on, I would be prisoner Rowe MP3660. My identity was reduced to a number. Throughout all of this, I couldn't help but notice that I was being watched. I could feel eyes scan me up and down and pierce my skin from afar. It wasn't until much later that I would discover why. The only thing I remained certain of, was that I was completely innocent. The injustice turned my stomach, as feelings of anger and powerlessness began to simmer within me.

Having been given my new name, I was escorted by four prison officers and a dog, through the prison grounds. We were headed to the infamous prison within a prison. It was probably the most secure place on earth. I had heard talk of it.

There was an iron staircase, at the top of which was an intimidating steel door. One guard escorted me to the door, and I waited beside him as he knocked. Security cameras glared at us from every angle. The slider in the door opened, and a peering eye inspected me. The door was then opened. I stood there, with the guard behind me, waiting for a command. The space before me could only hold maybe three adults at most. There was a desk, video monitors and an internal door. Nothing else. I went in along with the one guard that had climbed the stairs with me; the other three and the dog stayed at the bottom. The steel door shut behind me with a deep clang. My nerves were shot. I could see I was still being watched, this time through a thick glass observation window.

The internal door in front of me only opened once the steel door shut. I was then escorted to a cell. All around me prisoners looked at me with a mixture of fear, admiration and disgust. The way they stared reminded me of the looks I'd received when I first arrived. Clearly they had more obvious reasons to give me such attention now. The cell doors had big letters on them in red, to identify the category of the prisoner there. There was category A and AA, for maximum security, and E referred to an escapee. I was an A.

I was escorted to my cell without a word being said. The door was shut behind me. I was now an inmate. The enormity of this was sinking in and I felt sick to my stomach. I was crying so hard deep inside, but no tears came to my eyes. The cell was eight, by six, by ten feet. It was a soulless space, painted a dirty cream colour. The first thing you see when you enter the cell is the window on the back wall. It's not like any other window you would have seen before. It was a minuscule square, cut out of a concrete wall. In it were a number of layers, each of which restricted the light coming in. There was a layer of steel slats, crisscrossed bars, and a final layer of steel mesh. Not quite like the prison cell windows you see in movies, is it? There'd be no wistful gazing to the outside world for me. No looping my hands round the prison bars. None of that. Not even close.

A tiny fluorescent light was attached to the ceiling. Below it, the iron bed was bolted to the floor and topped with a beaten-up foam mattress. A wooden table and chair sat beside it. In the corner, a triangular-shaped cast iron shelf was welded into the wall, on top of that perched a blue and white plastic jug. There was a yellow-y stained, transparent plastic potty in the corner. Nothing was technically mine. All I owned in the world was what I had been given: two sheets, a blanket, a pillowcase, a plastic plate and bowl, a plastic knife, fork and spoon, a bar of Windsor soap, toothpaste powder and a toothbrush.

A big steel pipe ran across the back wall, and was the full extent of the cell's central heating system. As you can imagine, it was not very efficient on a freezing night – and there were to be plenty of those to go round. This was the sum total of my new world. I had never seen a more depressing place, slept in a more soulless room.

I sat on my bed and buried my face in my hands. The full realisation of it all hit me for the very first time. I wanted to cry openly but I couldn't. I cried inside my mind and it was so painful. My throat was choked, my head hurt, and I was so scared. I was locked in the jaws of this prison within a prison. Even then, I didn't understand what it all truly meant.

No one told me what was going to happen next. I sat there waiting for what felt like hours. There were no clocks; I had no idea as to what the time was. Probably just as well. Would it be a blessing or a curse to watch time tick away on a clock, isolated in a cell? All I had accompanying me was complete silence. What do you do? I'd never experienced the likes of this before. There's no handle on the inside of the cell door, so you can open it to ask somebody a question. When I was being brought to the cell, nobody would speak to me. I had questions, but nobody wanted to hear them. I wasn't being uncooperative at that point, or making a fuss. From the police that handed me over, to the prison staff, and even the other prisoners, they would all give me those weird looks, as if I were an alien. I would only find out later why that was.

I just waited and waited in that cell, waiting for the door to open. When it did, I remember a guard telling me to slop out. I didn't know what slop out meant. I just looked puzzled. The guard explained that I should empty my potty, fill my jug with water and wash my utensils. He showed me where to go. This was the start of my new life. I was hesitant to leave my cell. Horrible as it was, it was my only safe space. I did not know who I might meet outside it. I was the new boy, and I didn't know the ropes. However I did as I was told and took my things to the recess to wash them. Again the stares followed me. What did they know that I didn't? None of the faces looked familiar, but every single person in there would have been deemed the country's most dangerous and violent. They all had the swagger, and the confidence of experience. Compared to them, I was just a little kid. Intimidation set in.

I don't remember filling up my jug of water and going back to the cell, or the door being shut behind me again. One of the officers did tell me that I would be fed at a certain time, and that this would be my daily routine.

In my cell, the view I had of the outside world was very limited. The blocked-out window was useless, so all I was left with was a little, round, glass observation hole on the door. It was covered by a steel plate, a bit like the cover to a keyhole, which the prison officers used to check in on me. You would think the absence of activity and distraction might make it easy to sleep at night. It didn't. In the ceiling was a fixed red light that illuminated the cell all through the night, every night Another part of the security measures.

From time to time, they'd choose to keep the observation hole open. It allowed me to look straight ahead, but not from side to side. It was beyond frustrating, although better than nothing. I could see the other side of the landing, and the cell doors over there. I knew there were some notorious prisoners behind them, but I was yet to meet any. Every day, my cell door would only open three times: once in the morning, once in the afternoon, and once in the evening. The morning would be for me to do the slopping out. It was less than pleasant to have an entire day's worth of piss and shit sitting under the bed, waiting to be chucked out the next day, however I had no choice but to wait for the morning ablutions.

My morning routine would be: go down to recess and stand alongside five or six other prisoners who were all doing the same. Throwing all of our shit and piss into the same space. The smell was rancid but after a while, I hardly noticed it. I did, however, learn that there was a right order to do things, so that I didn't have to touch my cutlery with shitty hands.

Michael, now my co-defendant, had also been placed in a cell in this same area. We were able to socialise briefly during slop out, and also during the time in the afternoon when they would unlock the door for us to get our food. You'd take your plastic plate and bowl, and go to the area where the food was served. Two trusted prisoners would put food onto your plates, and then you took it back to your cell to eat behind closed doors.

Other than for slopping out and collecting our food, we were banged up in our cells for twenty-three hours a day. The one hour that I was allowed out of my cell was to go to the exercise cage. That is exactly what it was. A steel cage. To get there, you had to walk past the prison office. There was a locked door, and prisoners had to stand back and wait for the door to be opened. We were never allowed to touch a door, something that has remained with me ever since.

Through that door, a small, metre wide corridor led to a large cast-iron security door, which was even more intimidating than the others which lead to a short staircase. I once counted the forty-five cast-iron steps, which were boxed in with thick mesh. I couldn't have had much to do that day, or any day for that matter. These forty-five steps took you to the exercise cage itself, which was about twenty-five by twenty-five yards. This is where you could run and exercise, albeit it caged in and surrounded with barbed wire. We were completely alone, except for the guards who watched our every move.

We were allowed out there, weather permitting, either twice a day for 30 minutes, or once for an hour. Other prisoners would look down and watch. This routine became my life for the next fifteen months or so.

There was the occasional 'deviation', as it was called by the prison officers. This was when something deviated from the set routine of the prison. One such deviation was when Michael was allowed to share a cell with me, but this was only allowed because we were co-defendants and needed to discuss our defence. This was a rare opportunity but most of the time I would just be on my own.

One day, out of the blue, I was moved into F Wing, known as 'Fraggle Rock' after the children's television programme, an ironic name given to the hospital wing by us prisoners. 'Fraggle Rock' was a Victorian horror show. In the piles of discarded bedding, mattresses and amongst rubbish, which hung from its huge iron railings, many of the inmates were drugged to their eyeballs with medication, incoherent and staring into the abyss.

This was a completely different atmosphere to my cell block. It was staffed by mostly untrained prison medics, as well as prison officers, and resembled a mental asylum. Prisoners would be sent there if they were having mental-health issues or were thought to be likely to commit suicide. In reality, it was a madhouse. Most of the prisoners there were drug users, psychopaths, or just desperate individuals. There was noise all of the time. There were fires. There was everything you can imagine. It was like hell. It even made my old cell look inviting.

I couldn't help but wonder if I would get out alive? Why was I put here? I later discovered that it was because I had been in virtual isolation since I arrived, and they thought I might be starting to feel suicidal. I was not suicidal. I was sinking into a deep depression, and I was very angry and getting angrier. I was in this terrible place for a crime that I had never committed.

I should not have been there. It was here that I heard Jona and Michael calling my name through their flaps. It was good to reconnect with them. Jona was shocked to learn that Michael and I had been charged with murder. He told us about his police interviews, and how they threatened to charge him with murder too. Because of that, under pressure, he confessed to a number of different burglaries that he had committed, and a number of others that he didn't commit, just to help clear the police books. He had accepted his punishment and was resigned to spending a few years in prison. Michael, on the other hand, I noticed was very subdued, scared and just as perplexed as I was about his own predicament.

Up till this point, I was still unsure about the full details of the charges that had been brought against me, or the circumstances surrounding them. One of the trusted prisoners who worked on 'Fraggle Rock' was a bloke called Bill. He was being held on remand in Brixton for stabbing a man who later died in the midst in a drunken brawl. However, he was one of the few sane and sensible ones on the wing. He often came to my cell hatch with a cup of tea, and eager for a chat. He was the one who first told me about the amount of publicity my case was receiving, and how it had been front-page news. Later on, he kindly slipped a few newspaper articles under my cell door. Now it all made sense. All the stares and looks from every prisoner, guard or other in this building, since the day I stepped foot in it. The media had built up the story to such a fever pitch since my dramatic arrest that I was painted as a monster. There had been a running commentary since the very first day. I was headline news. If I'd have been the type of animal that the articles described, I would not have blamed them. It was convincing. Why wouldn't they believe it? Now that I was behind bars, the country could rest safely in their beds and celebrate Christmas. Now that I was in prison, everything could go back to normal. Except that I was completely innocent of what they were accusing me of.

I got to know Bill quite well. He became a prison friend and I was grateful to have someone to talk to. We built up a good relationship. He slipped me tobacco and shared the occasional illicit joint with me. He would talk about why he was in prison, and how he was finding it hard to come to terms with the murder he had committed. Our friendship developed and remained intact for many years after that. He was one of the first friendly voices that I'd heard in those two months, and that meant a lot.

After some time, I was transferred back from 'Fraggle Rock' to the prison within the prison. It was here that I met people like Freddie Foreman, who was the enforcer for the Kray brothers, as well as some other famous gangsters. They were all in this unit with me at the same time, and occasionally, when our cell doors were open, I got to meet and speak to them.

Back in the day, gang leader Eddie Richardson was the arch-rival of the Kray twins. But now, there he was, in the same unit with Freddie Foreman. They must have called a truce because they co-existed so peacefully. You wouldn't have believed that they were sworn enemies. They all carried a gravitas about them but, being a youngster, I had no idea who they were and the enormity of their reputations as yet.

To give you an insight into the calibre of people I was around, also in my unit was a Colombian drug lord, whose curly hair and moustache made him a Pablo Escobar look-alike. I also met some very notorious IRA prisoners. Two of whom carried out a daring and successful escape from the secure unit. Pearse McAuley and Nessan Quinlivan, members of the provisional IRA, were on remand in the secure unit, awaiting trial on charges relating to explosives and a suspected plot to assassinate former brewery company chairman Sir Charles Tidbury. They set the place ablaze, with shots fired from a smuggled firearm.

It was around this time that I learned about the third person who would become my other co-defendant. The newspapers and the media described the crimes that I was being accused of as being committed by three men, but only two of us had been charged with these offences. The remainder of the twelve guys who had been arrested at the same time had not been charged. There were still a couple left that were being held in the normal prison population.

I didn't have access to a radio at the time, but I managed to borrow one, and that's where I heard a news item about the arrest of another man accused of the M25 crimes. He had been involved in a high-speed car chase during which shots were fired at the police, although none were injured. He had tried to shoot himself during arrest, so far that was all I knew.

A week later, a big coloured guy was placed in the same unit as Michael and I. Our new co-defendant. This individual was dangerous, ruthless and had been charged with rape, firearms offences, aggravated robberies and other serious offences that were unconnected to the charges I faced. The most worrying thing was that he was being linked to Michael and I. At first, I was convinced that I had never seen him before, that he was someone I did not know. Then it came to me, I recognised him as the guy that I had once let into the White House to see Michael. He was a very dark, chubby man, with short black hair, a black beard and a stocky physique. He acted like a Jamaican yardie, not a Londoner like me. He'd been placed under close supervision and suicide watch for attempting to take his own life at the time of his arrest. He was clearly unstable.

When he came into the prison and became my co-defendant, my life as a prisoner completely changed. Now, I was being associated with a man who had been charged with rape. In prison, any kind of sex offence is frowned upon, because of this I went from just being an accused murderer, aggravated robber, and attempted murderer, to being a man charged with rape. Other prisoners looked at me differently now, and my life became far more dangerous. Now not only did I fear the system and what it was doing to me, but I had to fear the other prisoners too. I became further isolated, despite already being isolated for over twenty-three hours a day.

This meant that every time my cell door was open, nobody else was allowed out at the same time, because they feared I'd be attacked. Whenever I went into the exercise yard, even though I was in a cage and watched by guards, nobody else was allowed there. This terrifying phase of my stay in prison went on for many months.

One upside was that my solicitors and lawyers began visiting me more regularly. Having been denied the opportunity for so long, I was finally learning more about that of which I was accused. At this stage, I had still not seen any detailed paperwork, such as witness statements. The more I learned from my solicitor, the angrier I became. I was not involved in any way, in what I was being accused of. The facts made that clear as day, and yet, here I was fighting to prove my innocence from the secure unit of Brixton Prison. That is somewhere I should never have been. My anger drove me to fight back, and do whatever it would take to clear my name. This now consumed my every waking moment.

I knew that if I were to succeed, I needed to be both physically and mentally fit, therefore I took up yoga in my cell, and exercised as much as I could. Being locked up for nearly 24 hours a day, you need to keep your mind active. My parents sent me a small transistor radio. It only had medium wave, but at least it was a radio! This, and the occasional newspaper which was passed to all of the cells, in turn, was the sum of my entertainment and information. That is, of course, apart from visits. Whenever someone came to visit me, I would be escorted to a small private room by three prison officers. My 'high risk' status meant I was not allowed to receive a visit in a communal visiting area.

The first thing I'd have to do was take off all my clothes and be thoroughly searched. There was no such thing as privacy. During visits, a Screw would always stand close by watching and listening to everything, and writing down all of my movements. They did this using a little notebook with a large letter 'A' stamped in red on its front. I remember my first visit, it was with my dad, my sister Belinda, my mum and my sister Joanne. My mum and my sister Joanne were denied entry because they didn't have any identification on them. Belinda was only allowed in because she had her bus pass to identify her.

I've never seen so much anguish and pain on their faces. I tried to explain to them that it was all a mistake and that I'd been wrongly arrested, convicted, and locked up. Still, I could see that they were both very shaken, physically shaken, by the experience. Belinda even cried in front of me. The sight of this took every part of me to stay strong, and even then it killed a part of me deep inside that would never grow back. Those half-hour visits went very fast. It was more frustrating than I could put into words. It's one thing to see suffering when somebody's done something. It's another thing to see somebody suffer when you and they haven't done anything at all.

My mum came on the next visit, and told me that the police had searched their home and taken statements from her and my sisters. Anyone who wanted to visit a prisoner, outside of my immediate family, had to seek approval from the Home Office. If they did apply, they would get a home visit from the police, who would discourage them. It destroyed many of my friendships, and left me with very little support when I needed it the most. The simple fact is that a lot of my friends were petty criminals, and the last thing they wanted was the police paying them a visit. The only two people who weren't put off by these visits were Nancy and my son's mother, Claudia.

Nancy's first visit was emotional, but being so strong-minded, not only did she cope well, but she became my rock. She'd pay me visits all through my remand period and even gave statements to the police and my defence solicitors. She was the only one outside of my family who gave me that much support – yet she was so young, and it was all so unfair. I have no doubt that she was in love with me from early on in our relationship.

Life in Brixton Prison was still tough though, for many different reasons. Fellow prisoners like Freddie Foreman and Eddie Richardson were too old, and too wise to believe everything they read in the papers, but not everyone believed in my innocence. I was still experiencing a rough time from the other prisoners. Occasionally, out of the blue, a little joint would be slipped under my cell door. How the gangsters got marijuana into the secure unit I will never know, but they did. These little regular gifts would help make life a little more bearable.

Even after having spoken to my solicitors and lawyers, it had still taken nearly six months before I started to receive any documentation. For the first time, I was able to read the statements and the evidence that the police and the prosecution were gathering. They were mounting a case to convince a jury that I was guilty of murder, and a number of serious robberies.

Of course, I was not trained to understand legal documents, and quickly it dawned on me that if I was going to prove that the case against me was a total fabrication, I was going to need to educate myself.

I managed to get hold of an old copy of Archbold – the reference book on criminal pleading, evidence and practice. This is the main reference book for all lawyers and barristers. It was invaluable, and helped me to make sense of the torrent of papers coming my way. Now I was able to compartmentalise, analyse and study all of these documents, and the evidence that was being put against me. It was helping me.

More documents arrived for me to read, and these were from the victims of the crime. Every word on those pages made me angrier and angrier. As I read about what I had been accused of, my fury tipped over the edge. I read them describe the two white men and the one black man responsible for the crimes in graphic detail. They were talking about two white men, one with fair hair and blue eyes... and there I was, with my co-defendant, both brown skinned, with dreadlocks! Institutional racism within the police force would become a prominent explanation for overt discrimination against ethnic groups in England, particularly in London, following the racist murder of Stephen Lawrence in 1993. Here I was, experiencing its full force in a prison cell in 1989.

Because I had so much time on my hands, I read every statement over and over again, and made notes to give to my legal team. We were now twelve months into my remand, and it was only now that I was able to read all of the evidence, documentation and statements which were being shared.

I remember making spreadsheets a mile-long, stuck together with Sellotape, to track and then cross-reference, all the inconsistencies and mistakes. I went into so much detail, that it must have driven my barristers and lawyers crazy., but so be it. I was fighting back. I was not accepting my fate, nor was I going to solely rely on the lawyers.

I would bang on about the most minute details, which showed any level of inconsistency. For example, how could they say they found this here, when a photograph shows it's clearly not? I would then get into the details about the angle from which the picture was taken.

Why were the police ignoring this? There were so many contradictions, with one person saying one thing and another saying the exact opposite. All of these were crucial details that needed to be highlighted. I was doing all this on pen and paper. I did not have access to a computer. My cell walls and floor became my filing cabinet. In the end, it came down to just a few things.

First, there was no forensic evidence, because I was never at the scene of these crimes (what a surprise there). As logic would have it, you have to be at the scene of a crime in order to commit it. It pains me to have to explain this, but that was the position I was put in. There was also no scientific evidence linking my co-defendants to the crimes. No fingerprints, no DNA. Of course, again, there couldn't have been, because we weren't there. Thankfully, nothing was planted by the police at this stage. At the time I was charged, none of the forensic reports linked anybody with these crimes. Not one.

The only evidence they had on me was from a girlfriend and it related to jewellery. For the life of me, I had no idea what that was about. The police also found three individuals to give fabricated evidence, with which to try and undermine our credibility. They would go on to provide a statement, not saying that we committed the crimes, but that we'd given them stolen property that they had hidden for us, and that we'd also asked them to steal us a car. This 'evidence' against us, accusing us of these things, is what allowed the police to link us to the stolen car that was found at the scene of the murder.

These documents were riddled with inconsistencies. It was almost laughable. Dates were wrong, times were wrong and places were wrong. How any of this could be taken seriously, I couldn't understand. Every single one of these that I would highlight became another part of my arsenal to blow these lies and fabrications apart in my trial.

I started by reading the victim statements. The first one was by Alan Christopher Ely. It was dated the 16th of December. It was the day after the murder and the robberies had taken place. He stated that he lived alone in a YMCA Hostel in Croydon, Surrey. At about 4.30 in the afternoon on the 16th, he took the bus into Coulsdon to meet his girlfriend Sarah Starkey. They travelled into central Croydon, where they went window shopping on the High Street.

Later, around 8.30p.m. Sarah's father picked her up and took her home. In order to build up a sequence of events, I then went to look at Sarah Starkey's statement for corroboration, only to find that there was no statement from her, which was strange. She was a key witness, and yet I wasn't provided with a statement from her. Ely then went on to say that after leaving his girlfriend, he walked to Peter Hurburgh's house in South Croydon, where he arrived at around 8.50p.m. The two of them had worked together in 1987, were good friends and saw each other frequently.

They had taken Peter's car, a yellow Austin Princess with a brown vinyl roof, and driven toward Redhill where they wanted to look at an Audi car that was up for sale. Following that, they drove to the White Bear pub in New Addington, which served Alan's favourite Welsh beer 'Double Dragon'. They parked the car in the pub car park at around 10.40 p.m. They stayed in the pub till last orders were called, and then left in the car.

They had only travelled a short distance when the headlights picked up two people standing in the middle of the narrow road. They didn't move, and Peter had to brake sharply to avoid them. They then saw that the man on the right was brandishing a gun, and pointing it at them, holding it in both hands. The man on the left was holding a large knife. Immediately the car came to a halt, a third man who they hadn't seen up until now, pulled open the rear passenger door. All three men then climbed into the back seat. One of them said, "Face forward, do not look back, and just drive!"

On reading this, I became agitated. If the police knew this, and also knew that I had five independent witnesses who confirmed I was with them, several miles away at the time that this was happening, how could they have possibly charged us? It made no sense.

The statement went on to say that Peter drove the car for a short distance, before being told to stop and reverse through the gate of a field, then stop and turn off the engine and the lights.

Next, Alan and Peter were dragged out of the car by the three hijackers. Peter tried to make a run for it, but was quickly overpowered and viciously assaulted. They were then forced to lie down in the field and were tied up. Facedown in the field, they heard liquid being poured out, accompanied by the smell of petrol fumes. One of the men then lit a cigarette. The thought of being set alight had caused Alan to pass out.

When he came to, it was some three hours later. The car had gone and there was no sign of the three men. Alan shouted for Peter, but there was no response. He got to work, trying to untie the ropes binding his hands and feet, and managed to free himself in around twenty minutes. He immediately ran over to Peter where he lay, and removed the gag from his mouth. He tried to revive him without success. There was no heartbeat. He was dead. Alan ran down the road until he reached some cottages and was able to raise the alarm.

Later, a post-mortem would establish that Mr Hurburgh had suffered a severe physical beating with blows to the face, the neck and the chest. A single blow to the breastbone fractured the lower section, which in turn impacted his heart, causing heart failure and death. It was a terrible attack. I couldn't believe that I was being accused of such a crime.

Reading the victim statement, it sounded completely different from how the police would later describe the incident in court. This was a very stark story, in black and white, and although there was much more to read, I started to feel some hope, because not only had I not been involved, but the victim would help me show this with his evidence. The prosecution files had been compiled in sequence, so it was easy to locate the statements of witnesses. It was the sheer volume of the material that made me decide to cross-reference it all. It wasn't easy, but I certainly had the time to do it.

This so-called evidence only became more feeble as I read on. The statement from the Gentle's family given to Detective Constable Vickery corroborated what Ely had originally told the police. I quote:

"I was woken at around 3a.m. because our dog was barking. I then heard somebody in our backyard. He was calling out "Help, please help, please help!" I went to my bedroom window and opened it. I saw a young man standing in our backyard. He said, "I've been mugged." I then quickly put on some clothes and went downstairs and opened the kitchen door and let him in. I then showed the young man to the telephone and he dialled 999 for the police. After he had spoken to them, we went into the kitchen where I gave him a cigarette and a cup of coffee. He then started to tell me what had happened. He said that he and a friend were coming back from the pub and three men jumped out from the side of the road and stopped their car. He said they were all wearing masks. One was carrying a handgun and one a machete. One of the men was black the other two were white."

This was also confirmed by the testimony of PC John Patching of Kent Police, who was on patrol in the vicinity of the incident and was the first to respond to the 999 call. He took notes of his conversation with Alan, who told him: "We were driving back from the White Bear at about 11p.m. and three men jumped out, stopped us and said they wanted the car."

"What did they look like?"

"Two white men and a coloured man."

As a result, the police put out an alert to look out for two white men and a black man. So why, I wondered, did they arrest three black men? Why am I here? There was also a more detailed description of the third man from Alan:

"Originally, I didn't really see him at all. Other than a brief glimpse, when I noticed he was also wearing a dark coloured

92

balaclava like the others. This was the man who spent the majority of the time holding me down. I heard him talk quite frequently during the incident, and got the impression from his voice that he may have been coloured, but he had a South London accent. In addition, I would put him in the age group of about 25 to 30 years. The other two men who had the gun and the knife appeared to be the same height, which I would estimate to be about five foot nine. They both appeared to be a stocky build. It was one of these two men that I saw smoking the cigarette. One of these men also had a noticeably deeper voice than the other two. I would also estimate them to be of the same age, 25 to 30. The man with the deeper voice appeared to sound slightly older, possibly in his 30s. These men were also wearing dark coloured clothing, but I cannot recall any more detail. They both had similar South London accents. I can say that one of these men was white-skinned because I noticed that through the eye holes in the balaclava."

Back at the scene of the crime, the forensic officers began to comb the area for evidence. PC David Hills was driving a patrol car at the time of the incident. When he got to the junction by the field, he picked up the reflection of the rear lights of a vehicle in the entrance to a field. As he stopped at the junction, he saw that it was a green Triumph Spitfire with a union jack on the side. It was stationary, about 10 yards from the road, facing into the field. He assumed they had been in an accident, had skidded off the road and got stuck in the mud. He put in a radio call and quickly established that the car had been stolen three days earlier from Sydenham. I recalled being repeatedly questioned about a Spitfire car when I was arrested. Of course, I knew nothing of this, as I'd never seen this car, and had certainly never been in it. If this was the murder case, then it didn't look too bad for me from these documents.

This left me wondering what their case was really about. The details about this so-called girlfriend and the jewellery I'd given her then came to light. Kate, one of the girls I was sleeping with at the time, was interviewed by the police following my arrest. This was the same Kate who had once written me a love letter demanding I leave Nancy, and commit to her and her alone. She had told the police that she had received some jewellery from me that had been taken from one of these aggravated robberies. She further said that, on the night of the murder and robberies, after we'd made love, I'd left her and gone out at about 1.30am and didn't come back until late in the morning.

This was one of the most significant pieces of evidence in my case, but there was a problem with it. Five other witnesses said they were with me up until around midnight on the night of the murder and robberies. One of them was a solicitor's clerk whom I'd never met before.

Crucially, on the evidence of Alan Ely, the murder and robberies were committed between 11pm and 3am. on the night of the 15th and 16th of December. Fortunately, as it happened, I had a cast-iron alibi from these witnesses, who were happy to confirm I was in their house, and these were not friends of mine. Kate's timings also supported my alibi.

Let's spell it out to be clear. Michael and four girls, Paula, Siobhan, Tracy and Kate were together with me in Michael's room at 25 Lawrie Park Road having a smoke and socialising

94

on 15 December 1988 between 8pm and 10.30pm At about 10.30 pm Tracy suggested we go to her parents' house to get something to eat.

At about 10.45pm I, Michael and the four girls left and caught a bus from just outside our flat. Paula decided to go home, and remained on the bus when the rest got off. Tracy's mother Jennifer, sister Sharon, brother Tony and Justin Frost, a solicitors clerk, were all at the Pooley house when we arrived.

At 11.30 pm Siobhan went home. At midnight Sharon Pooley offered to drive us back to our flat, as she was also taking her boyfriend home. At 12.20am, after we had finished eating, we left. Kate, Michael and I were driven back to our flat, which was about a twenty-minute drive away. Before we left, Kate had popped home as she lived around the corner, in order to tell her parents she was going to spend the night at Tracy's, when she really intended to come to my place, to use drugs and have sex.

We arrived back at my flat at about 12.30am Michael went to his room and Kate and I went into mine. This is what we had told the police, and what all of the witnesses told the police. Kate and I went to my flat alone, smoked some weed, did a line of coke and made love for quite some time.

The prosecution said the fact that we were being dropped home at 12.20am, and the fact that at this time, the Spitfire was at the scene of the crime was a MYSTERY they had no answer for. The answer was simple. We were INNOCENT. We were being slotted into a crime we didn't commit by a racist system that needed to restore public confidence by demonising young black men who could easily be forgotten.

95

By the time we were being dropped home, the murder had already been committed, by at least one white man as described by the surviving victim, and had taken place some twenty miles away. The first aggravated robbery was already underway, and had been committed by two white and one black man according to the victims of the crime. These crimes happened at least an hour's drive from where I live. As far as I was concerned, you couldn't get a better alibi than that.

Despite this, I was still on remand in prison, awaiting trial for these crimes. How could that possibly be? Even the description of the perpetrators proved I couldn't be responsible. The more I read the court papers, the less everything made sense. I had so many questions I needed answers to. For example, why would Kate say that I gave her jewellery, unless the police were trying to link me with items stolen from the robbery?

There was one piece of crucial evidence that came to light when I was in that cell in Brixton. It was another love letter from Kate, apologising for lying to the police. In it, she wrote that she had been put under extreme pressure to make a statement against me.

When I received that letter, it was as if somebody had opened the cell door and set me free, because that's what I thought would happen at once. Her evidence about receiving jewellery from me was crucial. The police were also using her account of me going out to undermine my alibi; it created a smokescreen that would allow them to suggest I had left my flat after we had made love.

But as it turns out, the letter was not my ticket to freedom, because the prosecution refused to accept it. Devastated did not cut it. But why would they have? It completely undermined their case. So, after eighteen months of sitting in that prison within a prison, I was taken to the dock at the Old Bailey and accused of murder, three counts of aggravated robbery and one count of attempted murder. Even now, I find it difficult to talk about this time.

THE CASE AGAINST

"IN REALITY, THE PROSECUTION DIDN'T NEED TO PROVE THEIR CASE, ONLY TO CREATE ENOUGH DOUBT IN OUR STORY AND UNDERMINE OUR CREDIBILITY."

CHAPTER 5

The case against

The journey from Brixton to the Old Bailey was horrendous. In a prison van, there is no space, no comfort and no air. Animals on their way to slaughter get a more comfortable journey.

The police outriders were back, their blaring sirens parting the traffic to speed us there. Why did they need to make this such a circus? It didn't matter much anyway because the real circus was to be in the court itself. I knew I was completely innocent. I knew I was an hour's drive away from the scene of the crime. I also knew that the perpetrators were white and I was black. Finally, at the time that the crime took place, I was with five independent witnesses who corroborated my alibi. This case should have been easy. Open and shut! Needless to say, it wasn't.

To recap, four key witnesses were crucial to the prosecution's case. There was no forensic evidence linking either Michael or me to the crime scene. The forensic evidence, that emerged after we had been charged, pointed towards the other guys who had become key prosecution witnesses. The fingerprints found on the car at the scene of the murder, matched one of the white guys who had become a crucial prosecution witness. He was the only white guy in the case, the one with fair hair and blue eyes, fitting the description given by the victims.

At the time of my arrest, the victims had said that the two men, a younger one and an older one, were in their car, returning from a night at a bar. The young man described being hijacked as they were driving down the road. He said three men, one with a gun, jumped into their car, and forced them off the road, whilst the older man was attacked and died. He described this happening just after the pub closed at 11 pm

After my arrest, and after we had been charged and provided the police with our alibis, the young man Alan Ely changed his story at the request of the police. In his new statement, he claimed they were not hijacked by three men, but that he and the older man had parked in a field. They were performing sexual acts on each other. The older one was paying the younger one for this service and that earlier on, they had both been drinking in a nearby pub. All of a sudden, they were surprised by three men who dragged them out of their car, and demanded money from them, before tying them up. That was his new statement and the timing of the attack had now conveniently moved to later in the night.

The three robbers abandoned the Spitfire car they had arrived in at the scene of the crime, and drove off with the one they had stolen from the victim. About an hour and a half later, the gang broke into a house containing a married couple and their son. The son challenged the robbers and got stabbed severely as a result. He almost died attempting to fight them off.

The father described them as two white men and a black man, with one of the white men having blue eyes and fair hair, which he saw protruding from under his balaclava.

Later that same night, the gang broke into a third house, where the victims were tied up and robbed. They couldn't say for sure whether the men were white or black. The newspaper headline the following day said that the police were looking for two white and one black man. It was front page news – find these killers! Yet, despite all this publicity, days later the police managed to arrest and lock up three black men.

On the 16th of December 1988, the day after the murder, the police recovered a Triumph Spitfire car from the field next to the murder of Mr Peter Hurburgh. The police forensic experts examined the car thoroughly and found the fingerprints belonging to two known criminals: Mark Jobbins and Norman Duncan. In the early hours of 10 December 1988 – that's 5 days before the Spitfire was recovered from the murder scene – a young man, called Shane Griffin, met Norman Duncan, an old friend, at a party in South London. Duncan's claim of homelessness led Griffin to invite him to share his room at 25 Lawrie Park Road, Sydenham, South London. Mark Jobbins already shared this room with Griffin. Later that same day, the 10th, a Mr Martin Membury noticed Griffin, Duncan and Jobbins examining his Triumph Spitfire car parked in his drive. Two days later, in the early hours of 12/13 December 1988, Griffin and Duncan drove back to Mr Membury's house in a stolen Mini motor car. Whilst Duncan kept watch, Griffin forced the ignition and stole the Spitfire.

Despite the police claim that they raided 25 Lawrie Park Road on the 19th of December 1988 as a result of an anonymous tip-off, it is probable that the police decided to raid the house after the discovery of Jobbin's and Duncan's fingerprints in the Spitfire.

Initially, all the suspects arrested from 25 Lawrie Park Road (including myself and Michael Davis, who also lived in the same house) were suspects. However, Duncan, Jobbins and Griffin were not charged with any offence, even though they fitted the victim's descriptions of the assailants and had admitted to:

* Handling and hiding the stolen property in the flat of Jobbin's girlfriend.
* Stealing the Spitfire.
* Possessing the air pistol used by the gang.
* Dumping the Cavalier and Renault stolen from one of the robberies.

Instead, they became key prosecution witnesses for the police. Duncan and Griffin claimed that I asked them on 12 December 1988 to steal me an MG motor car for use as spare parts, but that they stole a Spitfire by mistake. Of course, this was not true, and Mr Membury's evidence that the three white men were examining the Spitfire on the 10th of December, two days earlier than the alleged request, completely undermined what they were alleging. The fact that Griffin and Duncan abandoned the stolen Mini-car they were driving when they stole the Spitfire on the 13th of December 1988, suggests that they had stolen the Spitfire car for their own purposes and not for me, or at my request.

At the trial, several independent witnesses told the jury that they had seen the Spitfire at times that undermined the prosecution's case against the three black men accused of the M25 Crimes.

Miss Karen Garrett, a school teacher, and her boyfriend Mr Malcolm MacDonald, stated that they went for a drink in the White Bear public house in Fickleshall at about 9pm on the evening of the 15th December 1988. (The same pub where Mr Hurburgh and his friend Mr Ely were drinking, before they were attacked and Mr Hurburgh was killed). However, on arrival, they decided not to drink there because they did not like the live band, and so they returned to their car, which was parked in the public house car park. As they walked to the car, Mr MacDonald pointed out to Miss Garrett, a green Triumph Spitfire which was pulling into the car park.

At the trial, the judge, Mr Justice Auld, said that if Karen Garrett and her boyfriend saw this very Spitfire in the car park at the White Bear public house at about 9.15p.m. that evening, the prosecution's case was even less plausible. But did they see that Spitfire? The reason the trial judge said the case against me would be impossible if the green Spitfire seen at 9.15pm was the same green Spitfire found near the murder scene, was because the prosecution accepted the defence case which had outlined the fact that we were in the company of Kate, Tracy and her family, at her house miles away, at 9.15pm.

Before the trial, the defence did not investigate whether it was possible for another green Spitfire to also have been near the murder scene at 9.15pm, because such a scenario seemed to be improbable. Following Mr Justice Auld's suggestion of such a 'possibility' in his summing up and the convictions, this issue became of paramount importance to the defence case.

Further enquiries made by the London Programme and solicitors (after the convictions of innocent men) revealed that such a scenario was indeed impossible.

Mark Hugall, who is area organiser for Triumph Spitfire owners, stated on the London Programme broadcast in October 1992, "In 1988 I was the Surrey area organiser, as I still am today. I've never seen another British Racing Green or any green Spitfire Mark 3 in this area, or any come to our meetings or even to a national meeting. Green was a very unpopular colour, as it is still today. The likelihood of seeing a British Racing Green Mark 3 is very low, but to see two on one evening is virtually impossible."

Mr Membury, the owner of the Spitfire and a car dealer, also confirmed that he had never seen another green Spitfire on his travels around the South East and London, and that is why he went all the way to Southampton to buy the green Spitfire. What would the trial judge, moreover what would the jury have made of this evidence? It is a travesty of justice that this information was not available to the defence at the trial.

Mr David Ivens, a witness who was interviewed by the police, also confirmed that he saw the green Spitfire abandoned in the field, two hundred yards from the White Bear Pub and the scene of the murder, between 10 and 10.30 pm. on 15 December 1988. This is just thirty minutes, before Ely changed his story about being hijacked at 11pm.

These two sightings of the Spitfire, at times when I and Michael had concrete alibis, were further corroborated by the evidence of a crucial witness, Mr Peter Fyffe. He stated that on 15 December 1988, he took his family and some friends to the Horse of The Year Show at Olympia. After leaving the stadium at 11.30 pm, he dropped his friends home and continued to drive home along Blackman's Lane. As he reached Skidhill Lane junction at 12.30am, he saw through his headlights a Triumph Spitfire parked in the field opposite. Mr Fyffe said the car was green and had a Union Jack on the wing.

The trial judge said in his summing up "The relevance of that evidence is that it marks the time of the arrival of the robbers, whoever they were, at the scene of their first offence that night. It is conceded by Mr Bevan (indeed, it is inevitable, is it not?) that the Spitfire seen by Mr Fyffe in his headlights as he drove home from Olympia that night, must have been this very Spitfire stolen from Mr Membury by Griffin and Duncan." All three sightings of the Spitfire pointed to the innocence of us convicted men. The robbers were in the vicinity of the murder when the Spitfire was seen by the independent witnesses at 9.15pm.

Who were the occupants? Was it Griffin, Duncan and Jobbins? Unlike myself, they had no alibi witnesses to show where they were during the times the Spitfire was seen by the witnesses. As stated by the trial judge, Mr Fyffe's evidence marks the time of the arrival of the robbers at 12.20am I would argue it was there much earlier on the other witnesses' evidence. Mrs Jennifer Pooley "had never met me or Michael before."

At the trial, Mrs Pooley stated "I remember an occasion on 15 December 1988, when Tracy brought some friends home. Those friends were Raphael, Michael and Kate. I do remember quite specifically the time at which Tracy's friends departed, it was at 12.20am I remember looking at the clock because my daughter Sharon's boyfriend left with them, his name was Justin Frost.

Mr Frost also told the trial jury that he did not know me or Michael and had only met us when we were introduced to him at the Pooley house on the night of 15 December 1988.
He went on to explain how he drove us back to our flat with Kate on the night of the 15th, arriving at 12.30am. Why had all these independent witnesses' evidence – which unequivocally proved that we could not, and were not in the Spitfire when it was seen at 9 pm, between 10/10.30 pm, and also when it was abandoned in the field at 12.30am – been ignored?

The Spitfire, abandoned by the robbers at the scene of the murder, had fingerprints on it that matched the blue-eyed and fair-haired guy, who became a key prosecution witness against me and my co-defendant. He was the only person in the case who fitted the description given by the victims, but at the time, no one knew that he was closely connected to the police. Except for the police, of course.

During the remand period, we had no idea that he was a paid police informant, who was paid a reward. However, this was never disclosed to the court. After the trial and convictions, the defence discovered that a £25,000 reward had been paid. They did not know who it had been claimed by or paid to.

The prosecution case relied on circumstantial and contradictory evidence from four key prosecution witnesses, without whom we three black men could not have been convicted.

In view of the nature and importance of the evidence given by these witnesses, and their potential motives for lying, knowledge of this reward would obviously have been of great assistance to the defence. It would've undermined their credibility to be able to establish such an incentive, because receiving some or all of the £25,000 reward, would have been a powerful motive to fabricate evidence against us.

A request to the police and the prosecution prior to the trial for disclosure of the name/s of the person/s who received the reward was refused. When giving evidence at the trial, all four key prosecution witnesses denied expectations of receiving some or all of the £25,000 reward if we were convicted. If the four key witnesses, whose evidence was strenuously challenged, received or were promised a share of the reward money, that piece of information by itself would also have been crucial for the defence to know and put before the jury.

In October 1992, January 1993 and June 1993 the defence applied to the Court of Appeal to request they order the police and prosecution to disclose the information about who received the reward. However, the Court of Appeal upheld the police and prosecution's Public Interest Immunity Certificate, so-called gagging order, to suppress the information. They refused to order the disclosure of the name/s of the person/s who received the reward. Both before and after the decision not to disclose the information, the Court of Appeal ruled that a failure by the prosecution to disclose the fact that the prosecution witness whose evidence is challenged had applied for or received a reward for giving information is a material irregularity which justifies overturning a conviction.

The convictions in R v Taylor & Taylor were quashed in June 1993 by Lord Justice McCowan, who regarded the non-disclosure of a request for a reward by a witness as plainly relevant to his credibility and therefore discloseable.

Moreover, when overturning the conviction at the Court of Appeal in R v Rasheed on 17 May 1994, Lord Justice Steyn said "As a matter of common sense, a request for a reward by a witness might have bearing on his motives for coming to give evidence. It must, therefore, always be disclosed by the police to the Crown Prosecution Service, and the prosecution must disclose it to the defence."

In light of these rulings, I wrote to the Crown Prosecution Service to request disclosure of the names of those who requested the reward. They still refused to disclose the information. Each individual case should be considered on its own merit, but the similarities between the evidence relied on to convict Rasheed, and that in my case, are significant. Yet the inconsistency with which the law on disclosure was applied in these cases is perverse. The same can be said for the use of a Public Interest Immunity Certificate to suppress information that goes to the very heart of witnesses' motivation in giving evidence.

Why have the Police, Prosecution and Court of Appeal continuously denied me access to the information regarding who requested and received the reward? A £25,000 reward was paid in this case but who received it? The Daily Mail newspaper who contributed £10,000 of the £25,000 reward was approached. They were asked if they would be prepared to investigate the possibility that the money paid by the Daily Mail may have been paid to accomplices to a criminal offence, and/or the actual perpetrators of the offences.

The Daily Mail Deputy Managing Editor, Gareth Burden replied, "The Daily Mail reported on 31 March 1990 that it would be sending a cheque for £10,000 to the Chief Constable Of Surrey, who would pass it on to the anonymous source who revealed where the three accused lived. If you have any evidence to substantiate your claim that a reward was paid to accomplices and/or the actual perpetrators of the offence, we would certainly examine it."

After sending details to Mr Gareth Burden to substantiate the possibility the reward had been paid to accomplices and/or the actual perpetrators of the offences he replied, "As far as we are concerned the money was paid to the Chief Constable. We do not know to whom the money was passed on." Despite the trial judge's warnings to the jury, they must have accepted the four key witnesses' evidence against us. Therefore, any relevant material that was not disclosed concerning them, denied the defence the opportunity to demonstrate that they may have been prejudiced, hostile or unreliable, particularly where a £25,000 reward may have been a powerful motive for perjury. As a minimum, to safeguard the rights of the defendants to a fair trial, in respect of the evidence given by the witnesses, the European Court of Human Rights has held that the 'equality of arms' principle in criminal cases imposes on prosecuting and investigating authorities an obligation to disclose any material in their possession, which may assist the accused in exonerating himself. Such a duty, the commission has reasoned, is necessary to redress the inequality of resources between the prosecution and defence. This principle extends to material which might undermine the credibility of a prosecution witness.

If the four key witnesses anticipated receiving the reward money when they made their statements and when they gave their evidence in court, then this would be motivation to implicate the three black men in the crimes, and that meant me! It took years before this 'material irregularity' resurfaced and paved the way for my eventual freedom.

I still do not know why one of the key witnesses, whose statement led to me being arrested, also led to me going to Brixton prison, to suffer all those months, and led to me standing in the dock.; Moreover, why was the person who did fit the description given by the victims, was not there in that dock instead of me? That is the question I have been unable to answer to this day.

Later on, in 1999, they devoted an episode of the BBC's flagship Rough Justice programme to my case. The question of the fingerprints came up in the programme. When the police discovered that the fingerprints didn't match those of the men they were holding for the crime, but instead matched a supposed witness, the easiest and most correct thing to have done would have been to go back and question him about why his fingerprints were on the car.

In all of his statements to the police, prior to them discovering his prints on the car, he made no mention of involvement with the car. Now, confronted with scientific evidence, he was forced to admit he had stolen the car with the two other white men, and had to push it at one point. He claimed that he did this for me and my co-accused. Rather than investigate these omissions, the police conspired with him to fabricate evidence. That's what had happened throughout the case.

When the evidence started to point away from us, the police would get people to give different accounts to confuse the situation, or create new information that could be used to challenge the facts. I was standing in the door of the court, waiting for my trial to start. The courtroom was packed and there was considerable media interest.

I felt pretty confident because my Barrister had told me that we had the best three QC's in the country. Michael Mansfield QC, who had represented the Guildford Four, and had been involved in some big, high profile cases. Gilbert Gray QC, who was a 'Rumpole of the Bailey' character, with a great reputation. My third co-defendant was Randolph Johnson and he had a reputable barrister as well. We were confident that with such a good legal team to present the facts and the alibis, it would be obvious that we were completely innocent. We trusted that the facts would speak for themselves. We were wrong. It quickly unravelled into a nightmare of a trial.

The trial went on for three months, and was eventually put to the jury. One jury member, the only Asian woman in the case, was removed from the deliberations. I don't know why that was. After the remaining 11 members deliberated, the jury delivered a verdict of guilty of all offences as charged. I just couldn't believe it.

Both Michael and I gave evidence. I stood in the dock, trying to tell the jury that I hadn't committed those offences. This probably backfired on me because I was feisty. I was determined and I was argumentative, and I was black. I didn't give a very good impression. They didn't like me, and it very likely contributed to their guilty verdict.

On my part, I wasn't there to be liked, I was fighting for my life and I was prepared to go into the dock and vigorously defend myself, and put the record straight about what actually happened. They wouldn't listen to a feisty black guy with dreadlocks and believe his story, over that of the police. At one point, I addressed the jury directly. I said to them, "Look in the dock. What do you see? Two men with dreadlocks and one black man. You've heard that the crimes were committed by two white, one black, so how can you continue?" I was reprimanded by the judge. In reality, the prosecution didn't need to prove their case, only to create enough doubt in our story and undermine our credibility. They needed to get the jury's sympathy for the victims and portray us as heartless thugs. The facts hardly mattered. The prosecution was clever in asking each witness if they could have been mistaken? Most replied that it was possible. That was enough to cast doubt on their evidence and for them to find us guilty.

I have to give racism it's due; it certainly helped secure that guilty verdict. The racial tension that gripped the nation in the 80s had infiltrated the courtroom. Not only were we fighting an element of racism, but we were also fighting manipulation, misrepresentation and all the things that bring about a miscarriage of justice. In the end, the judge handed down a sentence which consisted of life for murder, twelve years for aggravated robbery, fifteen years for aggravated burglary and fifteen years for attempted murder. That brought my sentence up to fifty-seven years.

In the British justice system, your case is reviewed by the Parole Board at various intervals. For parole to be considered, you are required to confess your guilt in front of the parole board. This I could not do. My unshakeable and rigid belief in my innocence meant I could not bring myself to do this. That meant I had a life sentence with no prospect of parole.

Immediately after the verdict and the sentence, I was literally dragged back to Brixton. In the courtroom, all hell had broken loose. How could a jury ignore the alibis and identification issues in our case and go on to convict us? We found out later that there was a serious element of explicit racial bias during their deliberations. No surprise there.

STATEMENT OF BR2543 ANDREW THOMPSON.
TAKEN BY RAPHAEL ROWE: WORMWOOD SCRUBS H.M.P

CELL4-62 "D-WING" DATE: 6 JULY 1993 TIME: 6.50 PM

I was on remand in Belmarsh Prison having been arrested on the 6th of February 1992. During my time held on remand,

I was being represented by Mr Jeremy Bull from Atkins Hope Solicitors.

During one of the conferences I had with Mr Bull, he told me about cases he had been involved in and one of those cases he mentioned was the so-called M25 case. He went on to tell me that a young lady had come to his office and said the reason why the three men involved in the M25 case were convicted was that they were black. He also added that this young lady was a member of the JURY at the trial. He further indicated that the M25 case was the hundredth appeal case on a pile of cases. I am not sure what he meant by this. I would like to add that I am not prejudiced against Mr Bull because I was convicted of murder and he was my solicitor. I have no reason to state that this conversation took place other than that it did.

I think it is appalling that he did not pass this information on to the men's lawyers. I passed this information on to Mr Rowe once I learnt he was one of the men accused of these crimes.

Signed: A Thompson.

Back at Brixton, my status had changed, I was no longer just on remand and waiting to be sentenced, but I was now officially guilty and convicted of all of the horrible crimes I had been accused of. The atmosphere and attitudes there toward me changed dramatically. Not for the better. There were now people who wanted to kill me.

Predictably, the newspapers and television news programmes were full of stories on the trial and the guilty verdict. I was a murdering monster. There were even calls to bring back hanging because of me!

The third co-defendant in the case, Johnson, I never saw again until the final appeal. I was only going to remain in Brixton for a short period. I was speedily moved to Wormwood Scrubs, a Gothic fronted building in the White City area of London, that had been operational since 1875. It was once described by the governor of the time as a 'penal dustbin'. I couldn't wait!

I was still a Category A prisoner requiring maximum security, but that didn't matter to me. This was going to be the start of my fight back. Not only would I survive this, but I was determined to completely clear my name. True justice had to be done.

"I JUST KNEW IN MY HEART OF HEARTS THAT THE POINTS I WAS MAKING WERE RIGHT. I MIGHT NOT HAVE BEEN ABLE TO ARTICULATE IT THE WAY I NEEDED TO. MAYBE THAT'S WHAT STOPPED ME GETTING THROUGH TO THEM. BUT I KNEW THAT WE HAD TO ADDRESS EVERY SINGLE ONE OF THEM UNTIL WE SUCCEEDED. I KNEW IT WAS POSSIBLE."

06

FIGHTING FOR MY FREEDOM

CHAPTER 6

Fighting For My Freedom

Having put every ounce of energy and determination into fighting my case in court only to be found guilty, I might have been expected to throw in the towel. I'd spent every hour of my existence on remand researching all the inaccuracies and scrutinizing each contradiction only for the justice system to turn a blind eye. You probably would've forgiven me at that point had I simply given up and settled down to do my time. That was just not an option. I cannot put into words how it burned me to be so let down by the system. Witnesses had been manipulated and pressured into lying. The whole process was rotten from the outset.

Hadn't the police done a fantastic job of tarnishing my reputation? It was a work of art. I fully accept that my life outside had been a string of bad choices. I was involved in crime and violence. There were times I did good things as a teenager, but generally speaking, I was not a nice guy. I regret it, and my remorse is a product of my own conscience. It's not because anybody told me to be sorry. But I was not a murderer. I didn't have the capacity to even think of committing the types of crimes I found myself convicted of. It wasn't in me. My previous convictions, my lifestyle and my disregard for authority were born out of circumstances. That's not an excuse, that was the reality for boys like me. I was a twenty-year-old leading an unhealthy life, playing the bad-boy and caught up in the same cycle that many before us, and after us, got caught up in as well.

That didn't matter to the jury. They bought the callous image that the police and prosecution painted of me full price cash-in-hand.

It begs the question as to how many other people the police had done this to. For how many others had they tampered with the facts and allowed to be unjustly convicted? This couldn't be allowed to rest or to be whitewashed over. Something had to be done, and I was going to do it. Even though I was behind bars. Wormwood Scrubs was everything you would expect from a purpose-built Victorian prison. It was made to be intimidating and it succeeded.

When you arrive as a convicted murderer you get treated differently. All other prisoners, other than lifers, look at you in a fearful kind of way. They know you've got nothing to lose. You're dangerous. I was still young, and my feisty behaviour had matured into volatility. Extreme volatility. The anger inside me had spread and manifested itself in the facial expression I wore every minute of every day.

There were a lot of other guys in the Scrubs who were bigger, bolder and more dangerous than me. These were actual murderers and violent offenders of all shapes and sizes. In order to survive, I had to take on some of the notorious reputation I'd been given by the media and give off that aura. I developed a presence that said, don't fuck with me; I don't care how big you are or how small you are. It didn't take long for that to be tested.

The landings from which you enter your cell were narrow. The day after I arrived at the Scrubs, I was walking down the landing when a guy who was leaning over the railings, stuck his foot out to try and trip me up. He spun round to confront me. I was smart enough to know that this was not a moment for conversation. I pummelled him with punches before he could say a word and I left him on the floor and walked away. But, in prison, everything has its consequences. I was hauled away by the guards and thrown into the segregation unit. Some of the guards took this as a reason to 'redress the balance'. They beat me bad. They spat names at me like 'murdering bastard'. They tore my clothes off me and left me naked and hurt on the cold cell floor. That segregation unit was a place I'd become all too familiar with. There began a cycle of self-punishment: a fight followed by segregation and isolation followed by a fight. But it was starting to produce the desired result. People thought twice about confronting me.

Most of the prison cells were the same in the Scrubs. There were always three layers of bars as a minimum. As a Lifer, I would always have a cell to myself. They don't put Lifers in double cells. I tried my best to make the little space I had my own. The moment you stepped inside, you could always tell it was mine by little touches. I used toothpaste to stick the one photo I had of Nancy on the wall right next to the photos of my sisters, parents and nephews.

My lawyers had told me that there were grounds for me to make an appeal against my conviction. I could've told them that from how unsound my judgement was, but I wondered if they just said that to everyone. Perhaps they were just trying to give me hope. Hope was what I needed. I was deflated after the failure of my original defence. The thought of going through all of that again for the appeal did not excite me. But I knew that if I ever wanted to breathe fresh air again, it had to be done. My life depended on it. I refused to give up on myself, but I did start to have serious doubts about my legal team.

My legal team's words fell onto a different pair of ears than the last time round. By now all my study and research have given me a far greater understanding of the law and the processes around it. I started to get the feeling that my lawyers were just telling me what I wanted to hear. I needed people who gave a damn about me. I needed someone who believed my innocence with every fibre of their being. Their their hearts just weren't in the outcome. Maybe they lacked the determination that I had. After all, it wasn't their life on the line. They could walk out the door, smoke their cigars and pick up their monthly pay-cheque no matter what happened. It didn't make much difference to them if I spent the rest of my life in prison.

Even during the preparation for my defence, every time I flagged errors, inaccuracies and inconsistencies that were crucial to the case, I felt dismissed. They led me to believe that I was being a nuisance and that my input wasn't relevant. Why would I trust the same team once again? I had some serious thinking to do. All the while I had to keep survival at the front of my mind. The regime in the Scrubs was brutal and I had to fight the system and keep myself alive. Neither was made easy.

I was constantly on guard for the unpredictable. Every day my cell door was kept open. I didn't know what I was going to face. I knew myself and what I was prepared to do. But I didn't know what the guy next door was going to be like, or the guy opposite me. Any guy that I was next to would've been a legitimate convicted murderer or had some other serious offence under his belt. He may well come into my cell with anger in his mind and found that I was the perfect punching bag. Staying alert all the time is mentally draining, but that's everyday life in prison.

I started my fightback. First directed at my legal team.

My armoury consisted of a pen, some paper and blank legal notebooks that I'd managed to get a hold of. These were the big blue books that a lawyer would use to take notes when they came to talk to you. They were made up of perforated pages, larger than A4, that could be removed easily if necessary. Every time my solicitor came to visit me, I would ask him to bring another book with him. Before long I had mounds of filled notebooks leant against the walls in my cell.

When I think back it is a bit ridiculous that I thought I could take on such a massive task. I was twenty-two years old in a prison cell trying to 'out lawyer-speak' my legal team because I thought I could. I can imagine how irritated they must have been with this cocky, dread-locked prisoner with a Cockney accent and prison slang, telling them what they shouldn't be doing.

I just knew in my heart of hearts that the points I was making were right. I might not have been able to articulate it the way I needed to. Maybe that's what stopped me getting through to them. But I knew that we had to address every single one of them until we succeeded. I knew it was possible. Each flaw would chip away at the foundations of the prosecution's case until it collapsed. That was the only way my conviction would be overturned.

Every prison has a regime, and the safety of place depends heavily on that regime running smoothly. I was a spanner in the works. The routine started at get-up time which was seven o'clock. Everybody needed to be up at a certain time to slop out and then go for breakfast. This was not a hotel, there was no "à la carte menu" or room service. Everything needed to happen by the clock or there would be chaos. Breakfast would be beans, bread, egg and, of course, porridge. There were no full-English breakfasts with all the trimmings here. Not even in our dreams.

The next activity was when prisoners were released to the workshops, cleaning detail or some other job. Trusted prisoners would have the honour of wearing a red armband, to identify them, and would only be subject to doing light chores such as gardening to keep the grounds looking smart. Then one lucky prisoner would have the job of the 'shit parcels'. They would have to walk around the outside of each cell block and clean up all the newspaper parcels full of shit and rubbish that prisoners had thrown out of their cell windows the night before. This prisoner also doubled as a drug trafficker. They were in the privileged position whereby their job allowed them to move drugs around the blocks by passing them through the bars from outside the cells. They knew what went in and what went out.

I wouldn't do any of these. It was out of pure spite. I wouldn't do what the prison system required of me and I didn't care. I should never have been there in the first place. A prison officer would unlock my door for breakfast in the morning. On some occasions, I would get up and get it. I'd then go back to my cell to eat it, kicking the door shut but never locked. I would never lock myself in. After I finished my breakfast I might get back into bed.

Trust me, my inactivity wasn't welcomed by the prison staff. The rules stated that every convicted prison had to work. At about 8.30, a screw would come to the cell. If you refuse to work, you get put on report. At some point later in the day, a piece of paper would slide under my door outlining my report and the reasons why I was on it. I must have had hundreds of these over the years. I would only be let out of my cell to get my food at lunchtime and dinner time while awaiting adjudication.

In simple terms, I had to go in front of the prison Governor to explain myself.

Those meetings were painfully predictable. I would be dragged to the Governor's office and sat down at a table with the Governor perched in the chair opposite me. The charge would be read out, "refusing to go to work", "disobeying a direct order", "uncooperative", all of that. The Governor would say something like, "This is your one-hundred-and-seventh offence for refusing to go to work. What do you have to say?" I would say nothing. I wasn't going to play their games. The punishment could be anything from three days of isolation or up to twenty-one days, depending on the severity of the offence. You can guess which one I got.

The next day they would take me to the segregation unit. This was a space often in the basement of a separate building where everybody was isolated in separate empty cells. I'd go down to the block, sometimes willingly but most of the time I'd let my body sag and have myself dragged down there by prison staff. When I said I wasn't going to cooperate, I meant it. I shouldn't be here. I'm not doing what you want me to do. Full stop. In the isolation unit, the cell would have a cardboard table and chair. Instead of a bed, there'd be a creaky iron frame which you could only lie on if you had the foam mattress. They would give me a mattress last thing at night and take it away first thing in the morning to stop me from lying down during the day. Not a friendly gesture.

They would also take the cardboard table and the cardboard chair in case you used it as a weapon. I never saw the point in that. Imagine trying to attack someone with a cardboard box. They'd just laugh straight in your face.

The guards found ways to create different levels of punishment depending on the severity of my offence. At one end of the scale, it might be the total loss of all privileges in which case everything would be taken out of the cell. Other times the punishment wouldn't be quite as severe. I might have those twenty-one days of isolation but be allowed to keep the mattress. If they were feeling generous, I might also be allowed my pen, notebooks and legal papers. That was a rarity.

Once the prison officers had cleared my cell, I was left on my own with the four walls, the tiny window and the iron bed. The Bible they left in the corner of cells remained untouched. The only thing I could do was to exercise, so that's what I did. I continued to practise the yoga I started on remand in Brixton. It helped me calm my mind and body to the point that I was unreadable to the officers. The rest of the time I was just alone with my thoughts and I had plenty of those. I was in mental pain that would never take a moment's break. It hurt so bad that I would just turn in on myself, becoming more and more depressed. Withdrawing from reality was my norm.

Days would come and go and as the years went on, I changed my tune slightly. I tried to compromise with the authorities. I told them that the only job I was prepared to do in the prison was to work as a gym orderly. That was one of the most privileged jobs. It'd be my responsibility to take care of the gym, including cleaning it. The biggest benefit to me was that I would have one of the most powerful tools in my locker to fight my wrongful conviction: the use of the facilities to keep my body physically fit.

It was a big ask for me to request this job. The guards weren't exactly too keen to hand out a more privileged job to me, the stone in their shoe for the last however many months. Then they saw it as a strategy. Perhaps by making me gym orderly they might finally get me to conform to their system, a task they were failing so miserably at.

They were right. Their attempts to punish me meant nothing to me. I had endured so much punishment, loss of privileges and time in segregation that it was no longer acting as a deterrent. I don't know how many days and months and years were lost in isolation and segregation. There were times when I was dragged to the block and the officers would try to beat the resistance out of me. They couldn't see it was pointless. Truth be told I don't know how I survived it. It wasn't easy. I would just retreat into my head and go into a zone. When they sent me into isolation my mind shut down, and my body went into neutral.

My resistance to the system was so great that my reputation followed me when I moved from one prison to another. The new set of prison staff would be expecting me to be a disruptive prisoner who protested his innocence and who would not conform to the regime. Some prisons took it as a challenge to beat that out of me. A few of them would accept me for who I was and would try to work with me to better address my needs. That was the exception. Mostly I was seen as a pain and a welcome opportunity for the guards to use whatever 'methods' it took to break my spirit and make me conform.

Sometimes two or three guards would open my cell door and insist that I go to work. I would refuse. They would warn me that if I didn't, I would be taken to the segregation block. I would tell them that I didn't give a fuck. They would rush at me and jump on me. Of course, they would class that as 'restraining'. Really, it was a cruel administration of pain. They would bend my arms and legs so I couldn't move and then drag me to the block. They'd kick me and punch me or bang me against the wall, knowing they could palm it off in a report. They'd write that I sustained the injuries as a result of my own resistance. You know, that I'd caused my own black eyes or slashed skin. I'd be stripped naked, thrown into one of these cells, and then left for hours, maybe even to the next day. After they might feel generous and chuck me some prison clothes to put on.

There were times when I'd engineer a session in isolation. Some of the other prisoners would be aggressive towards me and it got exhausting having to confront them every single time. I'd bargain myself some peace by running up to the guards, handing them an excuse to drag me down to the isolation unit. Whatever the reason, I continued to be awkward and refused to comply with the regime and my work on the appeal continued despite all the interruptions.

I knew the trial jury's decision to convict me may have been driven by bias or even racism. I knew they might have overlooked facts because the prosecution was skilled at manipulating the evidence provided by the police. I knew that I did not get a fair trial as a result of the prosecution hiding information and crucial evidence from the jury and public such as who had received that reward. There was even more information the jury hadn't heard that we discovered after my conviction and planned to bring in front of the appeal court. It was full steam ahead.

Later on in Wormwood Scrubs, there was an incident where I was very badly beaten up. I was in the punishment block after refusing to follow an order by a prison officer and I was beaten so badly by a number of prison officers that my injuries were too bad to ignore. I brought a successful compensation claim against them for damages. This incident, along with many others, eventually led to significant changes in the segregation unit. Not a moment before time. It had been barbaric.

Years later, the culture of brutality was eventually made public. My evidence helped to confirm what had been happening. The case affected the whole of Wormwood scrubs.

Even though I suffered horribly from institutionalised brutality at the time, that suffering didn't go unobserved. For years, those bruises and deep mental and physical scars lived with me. I never expected anything to come of it. A few years later I got a letter from a lawyer who was trying to challenge this culture and wanted to find out more. It gave me hope that there are people out there who really do care about what's happening to people like me in there.

"LIKE TWO GLADIATORS WE SIZED EACH OTHER UP AS WE CIRCLED EACH OTHER. THE GUARDS WERE AWARE OF WHAT WAS HAPPENING BUT STOOD BACK AND DIDN'T INTERVENE."

CHAPTER 7

Staying Alive

My short stay at Wormwood Scrubs had come to an end. I gathered my case notebooks and my meagre possessions and was, once again, escorted into another sweatbox for the two-hour journey up the M1, past Northampton to Market Harborough and HMP Gartree. As prisons go, this was comparatively modern having been built in 1965 on the western end of the RAF Airbase at Market Harborough. It had become infamous after a daring prison breakout that happened in the 80s. On 10 December 1987 at 3.15 pm, John Kendall and Sydney Draper were sprung from Gartree's exercise yard with the aid of a hijacked Bell 206 Jet Ranger helicopter.

Gartree was to be one of my more difficult prisons. For one, it was in Lancashire and so far from London that it made it difficult for my family to visit. The few times they did come became even more precious. The prison itself contained a lot of desperate individuals serving desperately long sentences. You know what that means. Nothing to lose. The day after I arrived, I witnessed a horrendous attack. I was sitting in the reception room watching TV with my back against the wall, It was one of the best ways to avoid an attack from behind. A young black guy, who had arrived at the prison at the same time as me, walked in and in a split second a group of prisoners grabbed him. They pinned him to the floor wearing makeshift balaclavas and threw a bucket of boiling water over his face and head. I watched in horror as his skin slipped from his face as one of the prisoners threw sugar at the pink skin left beneath it. I learned later that that barbaric attack happened because the guy was a convicted rapist. Needless to say, Gartree was a very volatile place.

There were a few people I shared something in common with. Gartree held many other prisoners protesting their innocence who were waiting to have their convictions quashed. There were the Birmingham Six, Winston Silcott, Gary Mills and Tony Paul, Yusuf Abdullah of the Cardiff Three, and the Bridgewater Four. I was in illustrious company. All of these men eventually had their wrongful murder convictions overturned and were freed except for Silcott who, although eventually released, remained convicted of a case of manslaughter.

The prison also offered activities to take our minds off everything. The staff had come together to hold inter-wing football matches for the inmates. My love of football had never once left me so I was keen to be on the team. There were four wings in Gartree: A, B, C, and D. Our fixtures every Saturday were A v B, C v D and every other combination you could come up with. The games were as rough and tumble as you'd expect from prisoners and, how conveniently, the referee didn't appear to own a red card.

Despite this welcome distraction, I had tunnel vision focussed on my case and clearing my name. I decided to put aside the doubts I'd experienced in the Scrubs and put my trust in my legal team. What other option did I have? On the side, I continued to fight tooth and nail to bring to their attention all of those inconsistencies and downright errors that riddled the prosecution team's case.

We had even found new and crucial evidence in the way of a statement that the police and prosecution tried to hide from us. The police statement was taken two days after the murder and robberies on the 15th of December and two days before my arrest on the 19th.

Statement of: John Malcolm Stevens.
Dated: 17:12:1988.

"Saturday 17 December 1988. At about 7.10a.m. I was walking my dog in Foots Cray Meadow, Sidcup. As I passed a wooded area next to the council burning section, which is a fenced area, I saw two vehicles parked. One was a white Renault 5 motor car and the other a red Vauxhall saloon. I noticed two men standing near the cars. One man stood near the driver's door of the white car. He, I'm sure, was white. Probably about 5'10" tall. I am unable to say much more about this man except to say he was wearing a full-length blue or black mac. The second man stood on the passenger side of the white car. All I can say about him is that he was also a white man. On seeing these two cars I realised what they were doing and so I turned for home and phoned the police. It is my opinion that at least one of these men must be local to this spot". This evidence hit the Sunday paper headlines.

"I CAME FACE TO FACE WITH MACHETE KILLER GANG" screamed the News of The World headline on the 18 December 1988. The article underneath the headline stated, "SHOCKED John Steven told yesterday how he came face to face with the kill-for-kicks gang and escaped. He was on a 7a.m. walk with his dog when he came across two men with the getaway cars stolen from one of the gang's victims". Quoting Mr Stevens, the article stated, "They looked up at me and I knew instantly that something was wrong. I'd seen an alert for the cars on TV and I knew these blokes don't mess around". On 19 December, the day of my arrest, the police took another witness statement from Mr Stevens. What you're about to read is a word for word extract from that statement.

"At about 7.10 a.m. on the morning of Saturday 17 December 1988... I saw two cars parked neatly beside each other... although the cars were some distance away, I could see that one was a Renault 5 and the other a red Cavalier... A man was standing by the driver's side of the white Renault car. He was looking over the roof of the car at another man who was standing on the passenger side of the white Renault... I can say that the man on the driver's side of the car was about 5'8" to 5'10" tall and he was wearing a full length dark blue or black mac... I am unable to give any description of the other man whatsoever".

These new developments raised a bunch of serious questions. Why after my arrest did this witness leave out the colour of the two men he saw and described in his original statement? Why weren't Mr Stevens' two inconsistent statements disclosed to the defence before the jury trial so we could expose just how racist this case had become? The two white men seen by Mr Stevens had never been caught so they have never been questioned or eliminated.

The evidence from the victims of the crimes remained that two of the three robbers were white, and one was black.

Could it be that the two white men who were seen by Mr Stevens were the two white men responsible for the M25 crimes? It is important to remember here that a victim of the M25 Crimes who described two of the robbers as white, said one of them had fair hair and blue eyes!

On 22 December 1988, the police pretended to arrest a white man, with fair hair and blue eyes, named Norman Duncan in Sidcup. Norman Duncan, you will remember, was involved in stealing the Spitfire and he became a chief prosecution witness at the trial. I call it a pretend arrest because it is common knowledge that this person was, in fact, a police operative and informer, the very same one who had led the police to the White House on the day of our arrest. To maintain he was not known to the police before the day of his arrest was a flat out lie.

When I discovered that the same two police officers who went on to arrest and interrogate me, DC James Gallagher and DC David Manhire, had also been responsible for the handling and pretend arrest of Duncan, the penny dropped. It explained a lot about why I, a brown-skinned youth with dreadlocks, had replaced the white man with fair hair and blue eyes. The conspiracy to fit me up was terrifying and signalled that this was going to be a long and painful fight.

One aspect of his evidence that Duncan admitted to was that he and the other two white men, Shane Griffin and Mark Jobbins, were responsible for unloading property stolen from the robberies. They took the property out of the white Renault 5 and the red Vauxhall saloon cars into the flat of Jobbins' girlfriend before dumping the cars at the spot Mr John Stevens described. However, Duncan, Griffin and Jobbins claim they

133

dumped and attempted to burn the two cars at about midnight on 17 December 1988.

Could it be that Duncan, Griffin and Jobbins were lying about the time they claim they dumped the cars?

Could it also be that Mr Stevens saw two of these men standing by the cars at 7.10 am? Had Mr Stevens' evidence been presented at the trial the jury would have had yet another question to consider. If these guys were dumping the cars from the robberies at 7.10am when Mr Stevens saw at least two white men, it further undermines the discredited and unreliable evidence. Therefore, why did they lie, where were they really and what had they been up to?

If Duncan and one of the other two white men were involved in the M25 Crimes and the dumping of the cars at 7.10am they would have every reason to lie! I seized on these crucial facts and filed a complaint to the Police Complaint Authority about the non-disclosure of this and other evidence including an organised, unrecorded interview with Duncan by the officers Manhire and Gallagher. An investigation was carried out by a subdivision of the same police force.

After the investigation, a report was sent from the Police Complaint Authority to the Crown Prosecution Service. The Crown Prosecution Service decided that there was insufficient evidence to prosecute the officers. The defence was denied access to this report due to Public Interest Immunity Certificates: the gagging orders. Why did the officers organise the unrecorded interview with Duncan? What was discussed during the interview?

Why didn't the officers record or keep any records of the interview? as Duncan promised a slice of the £25,000 reward?

The failure to record what took place during the interview was a clear breach of the Police and Criminal Evidence Act, so why were the officers not held accountable? The two officers responsible for the breach of conduct were interviewed by the defence solicitors on this issue. They told the solicitors that they had a "general" conversation with Duncan to put him at ease. However, during cross-examination Duncan admitted on oath that they spoke to him about crucial issues in the case. The conflicting accounts of what was discussed during the unrecorded interview between the officers and Duncan establishes one or the other is lying, but which and why?

The appeal itself was scheduled to take place in late 1992 but ended up being postponed and didn't take place until the following year in the Royal Courts of Justice in the Strand. Now that was a very imposing building. However, my legal team were buzzing with enthusiasm because between us, we had come up with several new grounds to show that my conviction was unsound.

My sisters' support never once wavered. It was around this time that Hazel and Joanne were being very vocal about my innocence to anyone who would listen, particularly the media. Impassioned by the injustice of my case they had leaflets printed "M25 THREE INNOCENT" and handed them out at meetings across the country. Their efforts managed to convince Trevor Phillips for the London Programme on ITV to take an interest in my case and make a documentary about it. The programme researchers managed to dig up even more evidence that supported our protestation of innocence. I was too scared to allow myself to get excited. I didn't want to be let down again in the same devastating way I had been the last time. But, emotions put aside, this mountain of new evidence coupled with the incredible facts were enough to make me believe that my appeal would be successful.

As one thing goes right, another goes wrong. My persistent frustration with my QC started to cause serious conflict. He did not share the belief that the new evidence was enough and seemed half-hearted in what he was doing on my behalf. He even publicly stated that he never thought that my appeal would be successful. I wasn't having it. Just before I was about to sack him, he resigned from the case. As a parting gift, he chose to cancel the appeal process. How kind.

It was a depressing time. The problem was that to get an appeal reinstated, you need to get permission from a single judge to confirm that he believes there are grounds for it. I was now on my own trying to battle my way through the legal system. By a stroke of luck, the Registrar in the Court of Appeal took pity on me and helped me to get a judge to endorse the application. I was able to recruit Michael Mansfield, who was already representing my co-defendant Michael, to take on my case. I was starting to recover. When the day came for the appeal I was once again escorted in a prison van to the court. Supporters, photographers and journalists covered the road outside the court and for once it felt like I had an army behind me. The stage was set.

It was Justice Watkin who was the leader of the three judges. I quickly discovered that he had very little sympathy for me. So much so that he dismissed my appeal. With one shake of the head, he decided that it would be a waste of the court's time. A chorus of anguish burst through the court. My family screamed in pain and my legal team screamed with disappointment. I snapped. My body erupted and I reacted in the only way I knew how. The screws wrestled me to the ground to restrain me as I spat fire at judges and the court. They pinned me to the floor and dragged me from the dock, down the concrete stairs and into the draconian cells beneath one of the oldest judicial buildings in the world.

Gutted doesn't even begin to cut it. I'd had such confidence that we would succeed that I had said my goodbyes to my fellow inmates and given away all my things. Yet there I was, sent right back the way I came. I was shipped back to Gartree to serve a life sentence and face the inevitable smirks and comments from the satisfied screws who had never believed in my innocence in the first place.

I found some escape from my suffering from other innocent prisoners in Gartree prison. I wasn't held in the same space as all of them but there would be a few in my wing that I could go and vent to knowing they understood. They were still fighting their innocence and, one by one, their cases went through the appeal courts for the second or third time and they won. It was one of my few sources of strength.

Two big challenges faced me after the dismissal of my appeal. One was hiding my disappointment. I was ripped to shreds on the inside, emotionally drained and my young hands didn't know how to handle it. Coping was a mountainous task and one I could only do while I was on my own in my cell. No matter how much pain I was in, I couldn't show it when that cell door was open. In public, I had to keep face. I'd tell everyone that I would get through this and I would fight on. It was turmoil and I even wondered at one point if I should seek some help to get through it. For some reason, I didn't. I drew on my internal strength. I firmly believe that this is what made me the person I am today. By acting strong, I became strong. I built up the thickness of my skin. I became more resilient. Fake it till you make it.

When you are on your own for extended periods with all of those conflicting voices in your head, you have to train yourself to be strong and listen to the voice of reason. You have to try not to give in to negative thoughts, and there are always plenty of them vying for your attention. Being positive is a conscious decision. The one thing I could always control were my thoughts. I could choose to look forward and create a new strategy to right this massive wrong, or I could look back at things and paralyse myself with the reality of those atrocities. I chose to look forward. When all other choices are taken away from you and you feel powerless to influence the events in your life, it's important to remember that, "It is never the problem that is the problem, it is what you think about the problem that's the problem."

Having had my appeal rejected I was now left with only one course of action which was to appeal directly to the Home Secretary. Only he had the power to refer a case to the Court of Appeal. At that time, the Home Secretary was Michael Howard who was a QC and had some pretty robust views about the justice system. His stance was summed up by his mantra: "Prison Works!" Howard repeatedly clashed with judges and prison reformers as he sought to clamp down on crime through a series of 'tough' measures, such as reducing the right to silence of defendants in their police interviews and at their trials as part of 1994's Criminal Justice and Public Order Act. Howard also voted for the reintroduction of the death penalty for the killing of police officers on duty and murders carried out with firearms in 1983 and 1990. Needless to say, he was probably not going to be the most sympathetic ear to my cause, but he was my only chance.

My legal team and I dissected the Appeal Court ruling against us. My barristers, my QC and my solicitor at the time called it a perverse judgment. Their words were as strong as that. Anybody reading the judgement who knew about my case could see it was perverse. The judge had completely dismissed the evidence that the gang consisted of the two white and one black man. He refused to accept the new evidence we had uncovered to reinforce the victim's descriptions of the gang. He also refused to accept the alibis and statements of all of the people I was with at the time the crime took place. These new revelations gave my lawyers a renewed energy to right this wrong and to get the case referred back to the Court of Appeal. It was set to be a long slog and it was going to take many more years.

In maximum-security prisons, there is a protocol about regularly moving prisoners to different cells to mitigate against the risk of escape. If I were to be kept in the same cell for six months or more, I could be digging my way out or even sawing through the bars. The fact that I was on the fourth floor didn't seem to matter, I would still be moved regularly.

One time I was moved, I found that the cell opposite me was home to a a big racist bully. It didn't take too long for him to take a dislike to me.

One day, I returned to my cell and I could hear a noise. I looked under my bed to discover a bird with a noose around its neck. By the time I was able to get it out, it had died. This was a warning – I was next! I was in no doubt at all as to who had sent the message but I had no proof. A couple of days later I returned to my cell again to find that someone had been in it without my permission and disturbed my possessions. An unwritten prisoners rule had been broken. This was too much. I knew I wasn't the only one being targeted, but I couldn't simply do nothing. That would put out the wrong message and invite further attacks in the future. It had to be settled in the only way possible. There had to be a fight and it had to be in public with other prisoners around.

My tormentor was twice my size in both height and width. If he had got his huge hands around my neck he could easily have killed me, so I had to outsmart him rather than overpower him. I went to his cell to "call him out" as tradition has it. I told him that I was fed up with his antics and that I had had enough. He lunged at me to drag me into his cell. I nimbly sidestepped him using my best Mohammed Ali footwork and told him we would fight in the association area, which is a big room with enough space for me to run at him and attack. This would be the only way I could survive this fight.

I knew that my life was in very real danger but I also knew that, by choosing to fight the largest and meanest guy in the place, I would get some respect and hopefully some peace from some of the other prisoners who were targeting me. It was a high-risk strategy.

The two of us walked purposefully along the landing and down the stairs towards the association area. The word spread like wildfire. A fight! One that would be worth watching! Like two Gladiators we sized each other up as we circled each other. The guards were aware of what was happening but stood back and didn't intervene. I was very angry and feeling very aggressive. I glimpsed the face of the bully and I sensed fear in his eyes. This gave me the strength and the power I needed to fight him, and the belief that I could conquer him.

I knew what fear smells like. I have experienced more than enough of it in my life. It doesn't come from somebody holding a knife to your neck, it doesn't come from somebody threatening you, it is an instinct that comes from deep down inside you when you know you need to protect yourself. Fear gives you great focus and a clear awareness of everything around you.

As soon as we reached the centre of the association room he launched himself at me. The difference in our respective sizes was obvious to everyone. He was at least six feet, a big build but overweight and out of condition. I was around five foot seven and very fit. I had kept myself in good shape. In prison, you need to be fit to stay alive!. The bully lunged at me with his arms outstretched trying to grab me, but I wouldn't let him hold me. Every time he grabbed me, I broke free. This annoyed him even more. The other prisoners were cheering us on, and the guards just let us continue. The fight became rougher and I became even more determined. There were cuts and there was blood and more besides, but we wouldn't give up.

We had been fighting now for half an hour and we were both exhausted. We had each given as good as we had received and were blooded and bruised. I believed that I beat him more than he beat me but I did take some licks, especially when he had managed to get me in a lock and I couldn't break free. It was a violent, probably the most violent fight I've ever had, and that is saying something!

Eventually the screws decided that enough was enough and told us to stop. I had taken on the biggest bully in the place. I had called him out and we had each shown no fear and fought hard. There was honour on both sides. Everyone was excitedly talking about what happened.

Frankly, neither of us had the strength to continue so we broke up and the crowd dispersed. I wondered if they had been taking bets. I went back up to my landing to have a shower and to clean my wounds. I was bruised and sore all over. The showers were never safe places. It is where you are at your most vulnerable. Never more so, than now. There are no doors as such, just the little Western bar-style barn doors which swing in and out. Many prisoners have ended up getting stabbed or injured in the showers, so I kept my guard up as you never know what is going to happen next.

Then I saw the big guy coming towards me. He was a mess and was also badly bruised and blooded. What on earth would he do next? I had practically run out of adrenaline after the fight, but somehow my body found some more. Was this going to be my final moment? I froze. He came close to me and looked at me straight into my eyes. "I have never known anyone to be as tough as you. You have my respect."

With that, he reached out and shook my hand.

That was the end of it. I breathed a sigh of total relief. It could have easily gone the other way. Not only did I survive the fight, but I lived to fight another day. From that day onwards my fellow inmates treated me very differently and with far more respect. If I could stand up to the biggest bully in the place, I could stand up to anything. In fact, that reputation preceded me as I moved in the future from prison to prison.' Don't mess with Rowe. He knows how to stand up for himself'. It generated an aura of fear around me which was a big help in the years to come.

"THIS LEVEL OF CRUELTY WAS THE REACTION OF AN APPEAL COURT THAT KNEW THIER LAWS HAD BEEN BEATEN BY A CLASS THEY RULED OVER."

08

HUNGER
STRIKE

CHAPTER 8

Hunger Strike

After three years in Gartree, I was moved to Maidstone Prison in Kent. It is probably one of the oldest prisons in the UK having been founded over 200 years ago. Originally serving as a county jail, it was converted into a prison in the 1740s. The main entrance was made famous by appearing in the title sequence of the BBC series 'Porridge' with Ronnie Barker.

Changing prisons is always stressful. I suppose that nobody likes change, but the regimes of each prison are so different that you never know if things will be better or worse. In this case, fortunately, they would be better. Before they took me to Maidstone I was sent to Wandsworth for an overnight stay. I still don't know why. They held me in a segregation block, and it was here that I met the infamous Charles Bronson. I was settling into my cell when I heard a tapping noise coming from the pipe that ran through all the cells to generate heat. I could just about make out a faint voice, so I crouched down to the floor and pressed my ear to the wall. It was Bronson. He told me he knew who I was and that he had respect for the way I was fighting for my case. I stayed there crouched and pressed against the wall as we talked for hours about everything and nothing.

The next thing I remember was being woken at 6a.m. for the last leg of the journey to Maidstone.

At the door the screw let me have a few words with Bronson who in years to come would send me some of his drawings and signed books.

It was the 25th of May 1994 when the prison van arrived at the gates and I prepared myself for the usual humiliation of the reception process. 11.15am marked the start of the next phase of my life in captivity.

Turns out, it was going to include some familiar faces. As soon as I arrived, I was welcomed by inmates that I'd met in previous prisons. Reggie Kray, who I'd first met at Gartree, was there having served 29 years of his sentence. On the face of it, Reggie did not have any more privileges than the rest of us, but his cell was enough to make you think otherwise. It was full of keepsakes and knick-knacks he'd accumulated over the years. Dream catchers hung from the walls and the room was dressed with curtains and quilt covers. Reggie had long accepted Gartree to be his home. In a couple of years, he'd even marry Roberta Jones in that prison on 14 July 1997.

The fact that I knew a few prisoners made the transition a little less tense, and that wasn't to be the only good thing about the move. The reduction in my prisoner categorisation from A to B was one of the things that helped me move to the prison in the first place. Now I was nearer to London and it was a lot easier for my parents, sisters and their children to visit me.

My sisters were doing everything they could to help raise awareness of my injustice, but they also had their hands full raising their own families. My eldest sister, Belinda, had three boys by now, Hazel had two boys, Joanne had two boys. I so looked forward to those visits with the kids. They were so innocent in a world that was so unjust, and their joy was a respite from the hardcore visits I would have with my parents and sisters about my appeal or how I was coping. The kids brought an air of freshness and I treasured those moments having fun with them and playing, just being a boy again. What it made me realise was that I'd never experienced that much love or affection. It wasn't just my family's presence that made this clear. In the visiting room, I'd see the hugs and kisses and exchanges between the other prisoners and their guests. I'd see how they'd shower their incarcerated loved ones with all the emotion and affection they'd pent up since the last time they'd come. I'd never been in love. I'd never even experienced that affectionate kind of love. Even with my parents and sisters, although I knew we loved each other unconditionally, we'd never show it openly or express it in words. Who knew it would take Maidstone to teach me that?

Although Maidstone was still an old Victorian nick, there was more open space than the other London prisons. There was a gym, a swimming pool and an AstroTurf football pitch. It sounds luxurious but, believe me, these were well-worn facilities that were squeezed into a minuscule amount of space. Having used football to escape the dangers and threats in Gartree I looked forward to doing the same here. I might even be a little more co-operative to make that possible.

It was at Maidstone on the 25th August 1996 that I organised a charity football match between my team and my non-biological cousin, Carl's. At the time he was playing pro football for Brentford FC. He came into Maidstone with a few squad players, some mates, and Brentford manager at the time, Dave Webb. Webb had been a legendary player and manager for Chelsea at one point. Jaws didn't exactly drop, then, when they beat us. We'd lost 5 – 4 but it didn't matter. We'd managed to raise a whole £1500 for a local school called Five Acres, for severely handicapped children. That was enough of a win. As a gesture of thanks, we sneaked a bunch of classic issue blue and white striped prison shirts with HMP stamped inside, to the opposition players after the game. We had them signed and presented by Reggie Kray as the screws turned a blind eye. Years later I'd do another one of these charitable games in Kingston prison.

A lot of the wings in Maidstone were full of short-term prisoners who tended to be more volatile. There must have been a policy about mixing prisoners who had short sentences with Lifers to add a bit of balance. In my experience, this didn't seem to work. Ecstasy was becoming a problem on the outside at the time and quite a few of these short-stay prisoners had been convicted for crimes connected to that type of drug. The other Lifers that I knew petitioned the guards to get me moved on to the other Lifers wing landing. Thank goodness they succeeded. This wing was a lot safer and quieter and Reggie Kray was on the same landing opposite me.

At Maidstone, I managed to bag my preferred job as gym orderly. The job allowed me to go outside and get fresh air and keep up the level of fitness I'd maintained since I first was put inside. I even trained overweight guys to get them to lose weight and helped snap the unfit prisoners into shape. The efforts I put into my physical development percolated into my intellectual development. I would also take courses in fitness training and continued to dedicate some of my time to study journalism.
I also managed to get some emotional respite.

Unlike in some other parts of the world, conjugal visits for prisoners are not available in the UK. However, for those in the know, there were ways. Without mentioning which prison – it would be so cruel if I did – you could appeal for a private visit on compassionate grounds if you received a "Dear John" letter. This was a letter from a wife or girlfriend saying that they couldn't take it anymore and threatened to leave you. In this particular prison, it was known that the prison chaplain would be most sympathetic to such a situation and help to facilitate an unsupervised meeting. In the prison hierarchy, a chaplain outranked a prison officer and had the authority to arrange for such a compassionate meeting. Over the years I was in prison, I had a number of people visit me: supporters, campaigners and journalists. There was also a consistent flurry of girlfriends that I met while inside who helped get me through some of the most challenging years. They were special and for their support and distraction, I am truly grateful.

I asked one of my girlfriends to write me a heartfelt letter that I duly showed to the chaplain. He was sympathetic and agreed to make the arrangements. The day came and I was escorted to the chapel into a small back room. The chaplain arranged for tea for us both and left us alone. You can imagine that with eight years of enforced celibacy behind me, I needed no written invitation to take full advantage of the moment.

There I was, in full flight, when in walked the chaplain to collect the tea tray. I froze. He said nothing. He just picked up the tray and left. Maybe the old romantic was gratified to see that our relationship had been restored.

This wasn't at all the case. Turns out he'd created a spyhole from the next room and had been enjoying the show. Not just ours, but every desperate pair he'd allow to meet in that room. He was found out later down the line, and if I'm honest I was sorry to hear, that he'd been removed from his post. Those moments alone with a partner were priceless to prisoners like me. I had now been in prison for 2,348 days. It was the 17th of March 1995.

We had some very sad news today. My heart aches for poor old Reggie Kray. His brother Ronnie was rushed in hospital yesterday and died today. Reggie hadn't been allowed to visit him before he died and he felt terrible. They had always been very close. Reggie was in my cell crying. It hurt to go in there and shake his hand. I felt a tear on his cheek jump on mine. Freddie Foreman, and Joe Martin were also comforting him. Joe was banged up next door to Reggie and he'd been in prison for about 30 years. He was another high-profile and notorious gangster.

They were both plying him with alcohol to try and drown his sorrows. He didn't normally drink. Later on, I was walking up the stairs at bang up time and Reggie Kray was behind me. He put his hand on my shoulder and I felt his need for support. Not because he had too much to drink but because the news was so terrible for him. And he told me he was okay. He said he feels his brother is okay now, he's at peace.

There was a dark cloud hanging over the prison that day for all of us.It took a couple of years to complete, but we managed to make a formal appeal to Michael Howard. It detailed every scrap of information about my case, all the reasons why it was unsound and how the appeal had not properly taken into account the full

150

facts or circumstances. My legal team had worked tirelessly to get it done and I was pleased with the result, but I wasn't going to be naive about this. I had no illusions about how receptive the Home Secretary would be or how he would react. The documents were sent in and we waited for a response. After some time, we received an acknowledgement that they had been received and were being considered, but that only meant they were sitting on a table somewhere gathering dust. It was time for a different tactic so we did the only other thing we could: lobby some MPs and get them to ask the Home Secretary about my case.

Paul Beresford, MP, was the first we approached on my behalf and I'd already secured the help of Edward Garnier from Gartree. Then fate handed me a stroke of luck. Ann Widdecombe was the Minister of Prisons at the time and she also happened to be based in Maidstone, her constituency. During an unofficial visit she was making the rounds and I knew this was my opportunity. I made a beeline for her and cornered her. You know, as politely as I could. I told her about my case and my innocence and to my surprise she agreed to go into the office with me for a chat. She was probably just eager to get me out of her face (I really had cornered her). Of course, that was against the governor's and the prison officers' wishes, but what were they going to say? There I was, sat opposite the Minister for Prisons, and I told her I needed her help. She was good enough to promise that she would make enquiries on my behalf. Now I had three politicians knocking on the door of the home Secretary on my behalf.

Ann Widdecombe was quite a powerful individual back then, and she kept her word. She not only asked the Home Secretary what was happening with the consideration of my case, but she also raised some other interesting questions on my behalf about the non-disclosure of evidence.

Before losing my appeal, a legal precedent was set in my case that had ramifications for the whole of the British criminal justice system. This centred around the disclosure and use of Public Interest Immunity Certificates.

These were certificates that could only be used, generally, in espionage or terrorism cases. They had to be cases where the authorities needed to suppress evidence because it was in the public's interest or for national security reasons. Yet somehow, those certificates were used in my case. They were the reason that information was withheld from my defence team. No doubt had that suppressed material been made available, there would have been a completely different outcome both to the case and also to the appeal. This was a big deal. At the time, several other big cases were going on, including one on arms-dealing, that were also riding on the disclosure of similar information that had been blocked by these certificates.

A person's "RIGHT to a FAIR AND OPEN TRIAL" had been compromised by the British court system. Judges now conducted secret hearings with the prosecution in criminal cases to decide if relevant information should be withheld from the defence. This secret hearing procedure was not a new law, democratically passed by parliament, but the result of a decision by Lord Chief Justice Taylor.

As a junior prosecutor, Lord Taylor failed to disclose vital information to the defence in the infamous case of suspected IRA operative, Judith Ward. She was convicted of bombing an army coach in 1974, and only released on appeal in 1992 when

152

the High Court found non-disclosed evidence (on a huge scale) that proved her innocence.

The High Court was so shocked at the withholding of evidence in Ward's case that it ruled that the defence must, in future, see virtually all the material held by the police and prosecution. Suffice to say that Ward's case became the standard that others would follow. Lord Chief Justice Taylor disapproved of the Ward standard more than most. He made it his agenda to change it. He got his chance to do so when he played his hand over my appeal pre-hearings.

My appeal was scheduled to be heard in early 1993, in front of Lord Taylor, however, it became a hearing over non-disclosure instead. Julian Bevan, QC for the prosecution, informed Lord Taylor of some information he wished to withhold from the defence but explained that he was not sure whether it ought to be disclosed. He asked Lord Taylor to make the decision.

Lord Taylor listened to Bevan's argument to withhold the material in a secret hearing. He saw the material and concluded that it was not crucial or helpful and that the prosecution was not obliged to disclose the material or even the categories of the information. The defence was deprived of the opportunity to decide whether they felt that the information was crucial and helpful to their cause. Therefore, I, my lawyers and the public were kept in the dark about the information. The same would happen in any other case that followed in our footsteps.
This was, and is, outrageous!

Even though we were held legally responsible for the conduct of our defence, we were not allowed to see relevant material that Lord Taylor, the police and prosecution suppressed using Public Interest Immunity Certificates (the gagging orders). Instead, my defence team were told to take the word of the police, prosecution and Court of Appeal that the suppressed information was not important. In other words, we were expected to believe the very people we accused of framing us.

The refusal to disclose the information using PII certificates carved out a rod for the system's critics to beat it with. After all, if the system thought that the information was not important, where was the harm in disclosing it to the defence and letting them make that decision for themselves? In just eight short months the Judith Ward standard on disclosure was reversed! The M25 case was used to establish a framework for disclosure which meant that the prosecution could apply to the trial judge, even in secret, for the court's authority to withhold material from the defence.

Basking in the success of his little mission, Lord Taylor then disqualified himself from hearing the M25 appeal. He claimed that he could not sit and judge the facts impartially having seen the material in question. At the re-scheduled appeal later in the year, a further hearing on disclosure was held before Deputy Lord Chief Justice Watkins. This resulted in the same conclusions, but Watkins did not disqualify himself from hearing the appeal. Instead, he dismissed it before retiring one week later.

It is important to mention that one month before my appeal went ahead, the prosecutor in my case, Julian Bevan QC, prosecuted a police officer involved in my arrest and conviction. He was taken in for conspiracy to pervert the course of justice in one of the most infamous miscarriages of justice, the "Guildford

Four". Disclosure was a key issue in the trial. However, in the case of the police officers, Bevan gave the information to the defence which helped the police officer's acquittal.

Moreover, at the centre of the arms to Iraq Matrix Churchill case, three executives could have gone to prison if the prosecution had been allowed to withhold information stamped with Public Interest Immunity Certificates. In a sensational move, the trial judge had ordered the relevant information to be disclosed. Once again, this disclosure secured the three executives' acquittal.

I welcomed the willingness to disclose information on certain cases, but something still didn't make sense. The information on these cases clearly had security implications. They dealt with information about the Guildford and Woolwich pub bombings, the IRA, and arms sales to Iraq. But the information was still disclosed. So, if these cases did not merit national security or public interest community considerations, how on earth did the M25 case?

The Matrix Churchill defendants and the former police officers needed disclosure to adequately present their defence and they were fully entitled to it. However, the same is true for me. I should have received the same consideration that the appeal judge gave the Matrix Churchill defendants and the former Surrey officers received from Bevan.

All this suggests that there is one law for the police and executives, and another for the rest of us. The use of the Public Interest Immunity Certificates was being abused and it was highly dangerous to the interests of justice.

The court's failure to act in an even-handed manner smacks of a two-tier justice system – and that is why I spent twelve years fighting. I waited for the Home Secretary to consider my case. I waited for six years and nothing happened. We got promises from his office from time to time, to the effect that it was being looked at but as the wait turned from months into years, I knew I had to do something dramatic to get his attention.

I then received a letter from the Home Office telling me that the Home Secretary did not intend to make a decision in my case but to refer the case to the newly formed Criminal Case Review Commission. They'd been lying to me for the past three years. It shook me to my core. I knew that had to be a purely political decision as Michael Howard had taken such a strong stance on crime and punishment. It would've been political suicide for him to to be seen to be lenient. I didn't fret. There's more than one way to influence a politician.

By now there was increased interest in my case from different journalists and media channels such as Channel Four. I was starting to see articles and features about my quest to clear my name. I was attracting attention, so how could I channel it to force the hand of the Home Secretary?

A hunger strike. It was going to be a huge gamble but what did I have to lose? My decision did ruffle some feathers in the Home Office, but they immediately tried to justify themselves with a series of faxes to the media. All their faxes achieved was to alert more journalists to my case. They were on the back foot!

Help from other sources started to flood in. My sister Joanne had been my soldier, support and the bastion of strength during the battle for my freedom. Joanne worked closely with

Pauline Smith who was active as a volunteer campaign press officer. Thanks to Joanne, Pauline donated her time by replying to the frenzy of media enquiries that were coming in. Some guys I knew inside told me of the publicity I was getting on the radio. In that instant, I gave Winston Silcott my mum's number so he could inform her of the pressure I was being put under. All the national broadcasters were asking for an interview, as was the national media. The momentum was starting to build.

On the 31st of March 1997 at 9.15 a.m. I went down to the senior officer's office after having a shower and packing the last bit of my belongings ready to go to the block. I handed them a letter which said that I was going on a hunger strike and requested to be taken to the isolation block.

They informed me that they didn't think my request was justified. I twisted their hand (figuratively, don't worry). I threatened to cause a disturbance if they didn't move me and out of nowhere, the Governor had the fantastic idea of locking me up in the block. I'd achieved the first step.

I was left in that isolation block with none of my belongings, except the socks, shorts and T-shirt I had on my back. Governor Bell, a young Scottish man would come in to check on me, as did the chaplain. I made it clear to them that I would not eat or take fluids. Pauline Smith came in to visit me one afternoon. We discussed strategy and she told me there would be a picket outside the prison tomorrow to highlight my fight for justice. It was being organised by a young man called Dan Waters who was also putting up news for me on this newly found platform called 'the internet'.

Once they knew I was on a hunger strike they tried everything to break me. The governor came in and asked why I wouldn't leave isolation and go back to the wing. He weakened and told me he didn't want people to think I was put down here by them. His only real concern was the bad press my decision might cause for the prison. I didn't care, so they raised the stakes. All of a sudden, I was presented with a succession of tasty dishes that far exceeded anything I'd ever eaten inside a prison. Out of nowhere, chicken, chips and peas would arrive. Then it would be eggs on toast with a glass of milk. I was strong enough to resist the temptation.

The senior medical officer Dr Nalanda came to see me one morning. He said he would be calling me over to the hospital to check my urine and weigh me after my adjudication. It was a much-needed break from the slow, boring confinement of that hollow isolation block. When the results of my urine test came back it showed that my fat was already eating itself. Dr Nalanda wrote notes about my health. I weighed 66 kilograms, which was just over 10 stone.

I had been on a hunger strike now for ten days. I was getting letters of support from everywhere. I did an interview with Robin Lustig for BBC Radio News. BBC TV was also covering the story. At last, we were getting some heavyweight publicity. However, I was starting to feel the strain on my body. Then, unexpectedly, on the 5th of April, my segregation cell was opened by the screws and I was told I was being moved to Swaleside Prison located close to the village of Eastchurch on the Isle of Sheppey in Kent. This was a fairly modern prison having opened in 1988 and it included a seventeen-bed health care centre.

I was double handcuffed to a screw and placed in a minivan with three other screws and a driver, plus an old man who was also being transferred. We drove out of Maidstone prison along the M20 motorway straight to Swaleside. There was no small talk. I just sat taking in the countryside scenery.

There wasn't much to see bar fields, trees, cars, a few houses and very few people, but it was more of the outside world than I'd seen in a long time. At Swaleside, I endured the same reception process, was photographed again, then led to the healthcare centre. The cell was small but much cosier than the block I'd been in. There was a single hatch on the cell door through which screws would give me a cup of hot water. There was a chair, a bed, a toilet, a sink and a locker. The window was low and looked out onto a small yard. The view was curtailed by a large white wall with barbed wire around it, but at least I could see some greenery in the yard.

The screws here treated me in a friendly way. To my amazement, one screw even put his hand out for me to shake and wished me well in fighting my wrongful conviction. I was completely dumbfounded. So much so that I shook his hand back. This was the first screw's hand I had shaken in all the years I'd been in prison.

That night, the BBC Radio Four's 10 o'clock News featured my fight for justice. The presenter did an excellent job interviewing the Home Office Minister, Timothy Kirkhope, and pushing him to answer the question as to why a decision had not been made? When would a decision be made? But I couldn't get complacent. The new Criminal Case Review Commission that was taking over from the Home Secretary seemed to be becoming quite powerful. It was making the news even in the middle of a general election campaign. A big achievement on a heavy news day. It was going to be an uphill battle to keep my story in the headlines when there was so much else going on.

A doctor and one of the medical screws tried to get me to stop my hunger strike. They pleaded with me and, as persuasively as they could, tried to explain the damage it was doing to my health. I refused to stop. I had come so far and achieved so much that I had to stay strong. Did I intend to die? No, I didn't. What I needed was to draw attention and publicity to my case, to my plight and also to the lies told by the Home Office and the Home Secretary himself.

Now something changed. The General Election was over, Tony Blair had come to power. There was a new Home Secretary, Jack Straw, who made a statement in the House of Commons. He said, "In view of earlier delays in dealing with Mr Rowe's case, he has been given an undertaking that a decision will be taken on his representations before responsibility for reviewing allegations of wrongful conviction is handed over to the Criminal Case Review Commission on the 31st of March." That's what Jack Straw said in Parliament – and then he did completely the opposite. You just cannot trust politicians!

It's the 15th of April 1997. The letters of support poured in in support of me and my strike. It was the solidarity I needed. That same day, I received a copy of the Criminal Cases Review Commission pamphlet explaining their duties and roles. What caught my attention was the fact that they offer you the opportunity to respond to their minded decision before they make a final decision. That had never been the case before. I then received a personal assurance from the commission that I would be properly listened to. So, on this basis and this basis only, I decided to come off my hunger strike.

Something else also was happening that was to make a big difference. The controversial question of the use of Public Interest Immunity Certificates in criminal trials was being actively challenged. Ben Emerson, a notable up-and-coming British QC, was building his reputation on challenging human rights law. He had become part of my legal team and was preparing an application to the European Court of Human Rights referencing the use of these certificates in my case.

While the Criminal Case Review Commission was still considering my application here in the United Kingdom, Ben Emerson was working in parallel pursuing the European Court. That decision came back in March 1999. The twenty-one judges made a unanimous decision that we didn't get a fair trial, and that the non-disclosure of evidence was against my human rights. This was the best news I could've hoped for and, more importantly, it placed a huge amount of pressure on the shoulders of the Criminal Case Review Commission.

To say that we have the best criminal justice system in the world is just not true. The British Bobby and Sherlock Holmes are myths – the reality is that Britain is home to a system prepared to use draconian laws or create principles in law that prevent the accused from reviewing evidence that will help their defence. At one point, the appeal court suggested my defence team review the content but before that they had to give an undertaking not to reveal or disclose what they had seen or read, not even to me, their client. Mansfield, who led the team, refused to be part of the cover-up and that gesture restored my faith in, at least, the integrity of the few who stand for justice and the doctrine of equality.

Another pivotal change now came my way. The BBCs "Rough Justice" Programme put a team of investigative reporters on to my case and it didn't take them long to uncover some facts which the prosecution had tried to hide. They made an extensive documentary about my wrongful conviction and were able to come up with many anomalies and questions that needed to be answered. It helped switch the public's view of my case.

I now knew that it was only a matter of time before it would all be over and my convictions would be quashed. Words could not express my relief. About two months later in March 2000, the Criminal Cases Review Commission told the British Court of Appeal to reconsider our wrongful convictions as there was now a sufficient amount of evidence to justify it.

Now, some of the arguments, if not all of the arguments that got our case back to the Court of Appeal, were technical legal points. It was about non-disclosure of evidence; it was about the behaviour of the prosecution and the police. It was also about my alibi and the discrepancy between the witness statements identifying two white men and one black man, and that the police had charged and convicted three black men.

Anybody who understands the criminal justice system knows that you only ever win appeals because of law, not because of evidence. Evidence doesn't win on its own, even if it's a forensic argument, because even with that you can never be 100% sure. In our case, there'd never been forensic evidence because we weren't there, but now we had the legal arguments that we needed.

By early 2000, I received information that my case was being referred back to the court of Appeal by the Criminal Case Review Commission. At long last, I had a date for the hearing.

It had been seven years since my last appeal, and twelve years since my imprisonment back in 1988. I'd served 10 years as a convicted prisoner and two years as a remand prisoner. Right now, that didn't matter. With all the blood, sweat and tears I'd put in, I had now become an expert on the legal process and, armed with all the meticulous research that I had started back in 1990 in Brixton, I could see the end in sight.

I was moved to Kingston prison at this stage and the developments in my appeal had turned me into quite the cause célèbre. Everybody believed I was innocent again. Yet, like many times before, I was still in my cell every day with documentation and the spreadsheets full of inconsistencies and questions.

Kingston prison was a place where everybody was a Lifer. It held both young and old prisoners and was a friendlier place than I was expecting. This was helped by the number of inmates there that I'd known from previous prisons. These guys had a combined time of several hundred years behind bars and it was like an awkward family reunion. However, Kingston Prison had something else that made it special. This prison was the only one in the country that had a football team that competed in the FA amateur league.

On arrival, they gave me a tour around the prison. I was dumbstruck when we got to the football pitch. Most prisons, if you are very lucky, would have an AstroTurf pitch just big enough for five-a-side. Here, right in front of my eyes, sat a full-size pitch with real grass. In my nine years of confinement, I'd never seen such an open place. It was heaven! I looked up and pointed to the windows that looked down on the pitch.

"Is that a screw's watchpoint?" I asked my tour guide.

"No", he told me, "we call it the directors' box. It's where the prisoners watch the match from when it is raining." Amazing!

There wasn't even a catch. The team only played home games – for obvious reasons! The only other slight difference was our goalposts. They were painted blue. Normally, the FA regulations mandated that goalposts be painted white. The only trouble was that the white walls surrounding our pitch made them invisible to the team. Permission was granted for the goals to be repainted and it was a compromise that didn't bother me in the least.

A lot of work had been done behind the scenes to get me to Kingston Prison and their football team. Before I even got there, I had to get permission. It wasn't just down to the agreement of both prisons, the Home Office also had to allow it. But Kingston's players had heard through the grapevine that I was a good player and, where they could, they tried to persuade the authorities to allow me to be transferred.
By some miracle, it worked.

After a short while playing on the team I was promoted to captain. The first season I was there, a journalist called Chris Hulme took a great interest in the team and our efforts to win the league for the first time after ten years of trying. He followed every match and all the players and immortalised our story in a book he called, 'Manslaughter United'.

Football was total escapism. Well, figuratively anyway. I

would spend all week looking forward to our Saturday game. But it was rough! The teams in the local league who played against us took advantage of the fact that we couldn't properly respond to a dirty tackle. They'd kick us and push us harder than usual knowing that we'd be put on report if we dared so much as to tickle them back. Being on report meant losing your place on the team so, as you can imagine, we were always on our best behaviour. Frankly, we were just happy to have the chance to play.

I only had one close call during my time on the team. An ex-marine on the team, who was also a good footballer, took a dislike to me. As captain, you can't please everyone. It comes with the job. However, I sensed that he wanted to take it further. I was right. On one occasion he came at me with aggression that could turn a man into a mouse. This guy was a killer and that darkness hung in his eyes. I had to make a split-second decision. I hit him square on three times. His feet left the ground and he landed on his back. He got up, ready to go again and so was I. We were stopped before we could go at it again, thank goodness. That incident almost lost me my position as captain, but I managed to cling to it. The trade-off for that was that my card was marked by the prison authorities who noted that I was still aggressive – even though it had been in self-defence.

As the end of the season rolled in, Chris Hulme's book was published and we were all eager to read it. We were totally unprepared for what came next. In that book, Chris had done something catastrophic to the team, more catastrophic than any kind of scuffle with an ex-marine could ever be. When you've done years and years behind bars, the politics of who's who is the last thing on your mind. In the early days, I made it my business to not associate with sex offenders and other types of prisoners. Many others adopted the same mentality. It became common law amongst us prisoners that after many years inside you don't ask about each other's convictions. It was just safer for everyone to get along in a confined space if we could communicate, even if it was on a superficial level. That's the only way it could work.

Chris broke this golden rule. In his book, he spelt out every last detail of the crimes of each of the team members. As I read, I found out that my main central defender was a necrophilia rapist. I learned that my mid-fielder killed his pregnant girlfriend. All of the team members, who appeared so normal in day-to-day life, were rapists and murderers. Once this all came out into the open, the entire team started to crumble. The ball wouldn't get passed to certain people and some players didn't want to play with others. The magic we had as a team had been shattered. This was a prison that built around its football team and one blow from a paperback book shut the whole thing down.

There are some things that I have tried to blot out from my time in Kingston. One of those incidents came on a summer's morning. As the gym orderly, I would often be unlocked ahead of most of the other prisoners to prepare the gymnasium. A handful of other guys would also be let out to conduct duties that needed an early start, like preparing food or setting up the visitors hall. In Kingston, the prisoners made their own ways to where they were going. You didn't need to leave the building as much of it was attached by spurs so there was no need for an escorting officer. I remember making my way down the iron stairway when I noticed what looked like trainers dangling in the air. At first, I thought someone had hung them up to dry after washing them, but I realised that the trainers were attached to feet. As I got a better look, I laid eyes on the full physical body of a prisoner hanging in his cell. You might ask how I'd been the first to see him hanging there. Prisoner officers would often open cell doors as if they were on autopilot. They'd prod the key in, turn the handle, push the door and, before they even looked at what was in front of them, moved onto the next. That's the only explanation I can submit as to why they missed this horrific scene.

In a blind panic, I pushed the door wider open and looked straight up at his face. His eyes were bulging out and his hands started to flap. As I grabbed both his legs together, he began to lash out. I lifted him up from the strangulation all the same and cried for him to undo the belt he'd looped around his neck. He did this and dropped to the floor. I couldn't believe what had just happened. I knew I could not raise the alarm. Even if I wanted to, through gasps of breath, the man told me he didn't want to. He sent me on my way, told me he'd be okay and said that he'd not try it again.

Later in the afternoon on my way back from the gym I stopped by his cell. I hadn't told anyone what had happened. I popped my head through the door. He was sitting there with another prisoner talking. I asked what that was all about, and he told me I was out of order for saving him. It was such a bizarre moment. I wasn't looking for thanks, I was just concerned for him and myself. Not another word passed between us until one occasion in the exercise yard when he told me I was the only person he knew that had ever done anything kind to him. We never spoke again. I don't know what happened to him, he was serving a life sentence for murder so he may still be in prison or worse for all I know. As work on the appeal continued, I had a new lawyer called Jim Nicholl. Jim was the first lawyer to 'get me'. His strategy was to firstly argue a point of law and secondly look at the evidence. We had been doing it the wrong way round all this time.

Jim knew how to handle me. He knew how to deal with somebody like me, who was in your face all the time. He understood my pain more than any other lawyer up until then. He was one of the first solicitors who took an interest in my family and he got me a new barrister, a new QC in preparation for my new appeal, which was now scheduled for May 2000. Jim had earned my trust

It was going to be a hard fight. The prosecution and the police were hitting back. They knew their backs were against the wall. It was like the famous "Rumble in the Jungle". We had to make sure that our boxing gloves were bigger than those of the police. They were. Every time we hit them it was hard. They were feeling it.

Besides, the times themselves were changing. This was the year 2000 and I had been locked up in 1988. The Crown Prosecution Service had just been created to deal with police corruption. They needed successes. A successful conviction for me being wrongly convicted and charged meant everything to them. It didn't matter who was innocent or guilty. It was about success for them to show that they were delivering what the public wanted them to deliver.

I was taken back to Pentonville Prison, somewhere I had not been for twelve years. Michael was there. I'd seen him over the years but only a few times. The last time was at our appeal in 1993. It was a long time ago and our relationship felt the full effect of the distance. We were two different people now.

Even though I'd been restricted, I'd learned so much about life during my time in prison. I was a very different Raphael compared to that young happy go lucky street kid of the 80s. The amount of reading I had done by working on the case had greatly increased my vocabulary. It also gave me a far deeper understanding of how unfairly the law served society. My attitude and approach to life had also matured.

Michael, on the other hand, found out that he had dyslexia. I had no idea. He couldn't read and write and so he couldn't process what I had processed in all those years. It explained a lot about his character. It had been a source of anger all these years that I alone was carrying the burden of the appeal. Now I knew why. Instead of being angry, I had sympathy. My approach bridged a gap that allowed him to start to open up to me about his own conviction. In those conversations, I learned more about Michael than I'd known during the whole term of our friendship.

Michael asked if we could share a cell to help us prepare for the appeal and the prison agreed. This was a new experience for me. I had always been on my own throughout my time in prison. Even though we had been flatmates before, that was a very long time ago and we were both very different now. I couldn't sleep at all for the first couple of nights just knowing there was another person in the cell with me. It would be a lie to say I ever settled into prison. At that moment, I still had deep anger and bitterness in me, not just for Michael, but for everything that I'd gone through. He'd come to terms with his environment. He'd done all the courses and all of the jobs. He was serving another sentence for a crime he did commit so he was set to do prison time anyway. That wasn't the case for me. The Appeal Court was packed with my family, supporters and journalists. This was the stage on which the drama would play out with three Appeal Court judges as the stars of the show. Both counsels made their submissions and the curtains lifted. I had seen it all before but this time I was certain of the result. Little did I know the judges were to have one final ace up their sleeves.

It was the last day of the appeal hearing. After all the submissions had been made, we all waited for the judgement. When it came it was not what we had been expecting. The judges made it clear that chances were our convictions would be made unsafe. But they were not prepared to give that judgment there and then, they would defer it until they'd written their report.

A shock ran through the court. This was just the diminishing wickedness of the legal system having its last laugh at my expense. This level of cruelty was the reaction of an appeal court that knew their laws had been beaten by a class that they ruled over. As a result, instead of me being released to enjoy my freedom, I had to return to prison whilst they wrote their judgement. One thing was for sure, they would be in no hurry to write the very thing that showed the police to be faulty and corrupt.

Like last time, I'd been so confident of the outcome that I had given away all of my possessions to fellow prisoners. But here I was, being escorted once again into the prison van to be locked back up. This time it was to be Kingston Prison. I was on my own with no other prisoners, just two guards who watched over me. In my mind, it was going to be the most painful sweatbox of a journey that I had ever made to Portsmouth.

As it happened, the guards in question were not prison staff but civilian staff employed by G4S. They were friendly compared to the confrontational prison guards I'd grown accustomed to. I remember one of the guards coming to the mesh window of my cubicle to ask if I was hungry. I replied that I was. They said that they were going to stop at a McDonald's. I hadn't seen McDonald's for at least 12 years but there we were, pulling into a car park right under a massive yellow 'M'.

Normally, there's a security plan that kicks into action during a stop on a transfer, for fear of escape. A prison transfer would go from point A to point B without any stops. This did not seem to have been implemented. I started to get slightly apprehensive, but my heart started to pound in anticipation of freedom I had not experienced for a very long time.

They asked me what I wanted. I asked them to get me a quarter pounder with cheese, strawberry milkshake, some French fries and an apple pie. Then the weirdest thing happened. When they came back with the food, they unlocked the main prison van in the car park, opened the cubicle door of the box I was in and allowed me to step outside to sit on the steps of the van to eat the McDonald's. I was a big guy by then. Years of dedication to a strict fitness regime had made me strong. I could have easily overpowered the guards and made a run for it. But what if this was a set-up? What if they were hoping I would escape so they could tell the public I was a dangerous escapee which would have a dramatic effect on my upcoming appeal decision. Escape did cross my mind, but being so near to release, I would have thrown away all of the years of deprivation and suffering. It wasn't worth it.

I just sat there, and I ate my McDonald's. The moment passed as quickly as it came, and I was put back in that sweatbox to continue the journey to Portsmouth. I arrived back in prison where everyone had wished me well on leaving. Now the judgement had been reserved and I was back, nobody could look me in the eye. I was just another prisoner whose appeal had been rejected so, obviously, I must have been guilty all along. It was such a disheartening, horrible, horrible feeling for me, and for some of the prisoners that I'd got to know pretty well. To be honest, after such a let-down I started to have real doubts about whether I would ever be free.

By now, they had started to put televisions into the cells. I'd spend days zoning out of my reality by watching Euro 2000. The zone of escape it gave me helped me to overcome the torment. I had no idea when the judges would complete their report and when I would be called back into court. This was psychological torture of the worst kind.

They announced it in their own good time. My appeal had been successful, and I finally knew this was going to be my last day in court. It had taken so long to come. The twelve-year process to clear my name had taken me through so many highs and lows that by now I was just exhausted. I only wanted to get my life back and slowly rebuild myself. I have been damaged both physically and mentally in ways I am only now understanding. My recovery and healing need time and still do.

That is not to ignore how much I'd grown. I had come through this with a mental strength I didn't know I had in me. I never gave up. I had never felt I was a victim. I had fought for the truth every single day of those twelve long years. My anger at the injustice that had been shown me gave me the strength to continue, bit by bit. If I was able to fight the system and win with only paper and a pen, there was now nothing I could not achieve. I was ready for whatever was to come next.

A SECOND CHANCE AT LIFE

"AS WE STOOD STILL ON DIFFERENT PLATFORMS, WE CAUGHT EACH OTHER'S EYES AS WE LOOKED OVER THE TRACKS. SEPARATED AGAIN BY STEEL BARS. MY BACK POCKET BUZZED. SHE'D TEXTED ME. MY HEART JUMPED AND, AT THAT MOMENT I KNEW SOMETHING SPECIAL WAS ABOUT TO HAPPEN."

CHAPTER 9

Second Chance at Life

Moving back into the real world after twelve years was strange. A lot had changed and so had I. I realised how institutionalised I was. It would be little things, subtleties in my character, things you might not even pick up on if we were around each other. Time and time again they'd crop up. When I'd walk up to a door, I'd wait for someone to open it for me. It sounds silly, but I hadn't been allowed to touch a door in over a decade. Anytime that I was away from home, I always made sure my back was against a wall. It didn't matter whether I was going out for a coffee or to a restaurant, that's how I knew I was safe. A wall can't attack me. In prison, I'd always slept with a lump of wood, batteries in socks, anything that I could use to defend myself from an attack. When I first came out, I'd tape masking tape around the end of an iron bar and push it down the side of my bed. Twenty years on, that bar's still there. So deep are those scars that it took a real effort to overcome these habits.

The internet was a whole other story. It took forever and a day for me to wrap my head around it. Mobile phones hadn't even existed when I got put inside so you can imagine how weird it must have been for me. Technology as a whole had advanced in such a way that I felt so clumsy and awkward moving through life. My parents and my sisters were my rock. With their patience, I was able to lay down those first bricks in building myself back up. I got to know my nephews, who by now had sprouted up into young boys, and spent my time with them playing catch up for all the years I'd missed. It didn't change the fact that I had no one to call my own.

During those twelve years in prison, my life went 'on hold'. In my mind, I was still twenty. I was actually thirty-two when I was released. In the outside world, everything had moved on during that time. But there I was, without even an inkling of what it was like to fall in love. My thoughts turned to Nancy. Not once in prison had I taken down her photo, no matter what prison I was being held in. Had she moved on? Did she even remember me now? I needed to know.

Here I was, a tough, brave, battle-scarred, old ex-prisoner and I was scared to call her to find out. I was even more scared to call her Mum! You remember that slap, don't you? So I got my sister to do it. Perks of being a younger brother. I'd heard through the grapevine that Nancy had recently broken up with her current boyfriend and was living back at home so Hazel rang Nancy's mum's house to see if she'd meet me. The message came back no, she's moved on, she doesn't want anything to do with me. Oh well, I thought. That's that! But a few days later, my sister got a call back from Nancy saying that she just might be willing to meet me. On an August day about a month after my release, we arranged to meet at her workplace which was in London Bridge.

In my mind, I was expecting to see the same sixteen-year-old that I remembered from twelve years ago. That was the girl who had been in my photo all these years and I'd not been given a more recent one to replace it. Maybe she had changed? I won't kid you and say I wasn't nervous, but it was the excitement that overpowered me that day. I was certainly older, wiser and deeply scarred by my experiences. I know I wasn't the same person that she would have remembered. But, at heart, I was still twenty years old. Here I was back and living my life.

I saw her step out of her office and make her way towards me. She hadn't changed a bit. Of course, she'd aged some, but she still had that trademark bounce of hers that I'd always been so attracted to. It was her walk as much as her personality and physical appearance. We found a table and it was there that the first words we said to each other in twelve years passed through our lips.

Trust me, that wasn't as seamless as you might be imagining. It wasn't long before we realised that I'd lost the art of conversation. It made sense; I'd been deprived of it for so long. But somehow, we managed to get through that time. I would just let her talk. It was like those years long ago when we'd be in my flat and I'd just lie there, content, listening to her. Like old times, she told me about her life and her experiences. My gut told me that there was still that chemistry between us that had been kindled twelve years ago. It drove me to be bold so when our time came to an end, I tried to ask for her number. She wouldn't give it to me. She'd only allow me to give her mine. It was a swift goodbye at the barriers in London Bridge station and parted ways to take separate trains back home. As we stood on different platforms, we caught each other's eyes as we looked over the tracks. Separated again by steel bars. My back pocket buzzed. She'd texted me.

My heart jumped and, at that moment, I knew something special was about to happen. About a week later, she invited me to meet her in Brighton where she'd studied at university. I met her, her sister and her sister's boyfriend at Bromley South station and off we went. That trip was the restart of our relationship. We picked up exactly where we left off as if I hadn't ever left. I soon had my own flat in south-east London and it wasn't long before Nancy came to stay with me. The rest, as they say, is history.

Our romance was as real as they get. We travelled the world and I fell in love for the very first time at thirty-three. Four years later our son, Jay, was born and I fell in love for a second time. I was the most doting father and I was so proud that I could be there to watch my son grow up that my heart could've burst.

In 2007, Nancy and I travelled to Jamaica to get married. Her dad lived there with his wife, Nancy's step-sister and her daughter, Millie. Jay and Millie were only weeks apart in age and the two had the very big-kid job of being ring bearers at our ceremony. The big day came but just before they could make it down the aisle, the tots got caught up in a moment of play and dropped our rings in the sand. It couldn't have gone off without a hitch now, could it? After a few panicked moments scrambling in the sand, the rings were found. We finally got to say I do.

I didn't think I had any more room for love but then, in 2008, Rosie was born. I had a daughter. My life was complete. I was happy and I was working. I was going on amazing holidays and earning a good living. I led a life that didn't even exist in my wildest dreams in prison and I protected it fiercely. I made a commitment to myself after my kids were born never to miss their birthdays, any school activity or play or any other public holidays, like Christmas. That was family time. The domestic and international travel that comes with my job has never made that easy but I'm a stubborn man if nothing else. I kept my promise and I celebrate these moments with them every year, even if I did miss my own birthday celebration on one occasion! The dangerous nature of investigative journalism meant I also had to keep the public's knowledge of my family at bay. I never mentioned them in public or posted images on social media with them. It's a hard thing to do when you love them the way I do, all I want to do is show the world the smiles of theirs that make me smile every day.

Still, those sacrifices were not the hardest thing I had to do as a parent. Jay and Rosie were growing up and I was now faced with the task of telling them about my past. My son was ten when I told him. We were on a family break, but Jay wanted to play in a football match for his team, so I took him home a day early. It was just the two of us. That evening, I sat him on my bed and showed him a few old newspaper cuttings of me being released from the court and the headlines declaring my innocence. His blue eyes stared at me in bewilderment, but he stayed calm, only breaking his silence to ask a few matter-of-fact questions. If I thought prison was tough, then nothing could've prepared me for that moment. I had no idea how he'd react so we had a very grown-up chat about what his friends might say and how he could deal with that whenever it did come up. I only had his attention for an hour before he turned his focus on something else. I was still scared about how he took it but   his sharp wit came back to assure me that he was doing just fine.

I was cross with him for doing something and before I could get another word in he came back at me with, "I didn't do it dad and you know what it's like to be accused of something you didn't do". How do you come back from that?

A few years later, I had to repeat the moment with my little girl, Rosie. This time it was almost forced on me sooner than I was prepared for. I had been recruited as a reporter for the BBC prime time magazine show, the One Show, and my first report was going out. It was a piece about Brixton prison and rehabilitation during which I referenced my own time there. I knew for a fact that some of my daughter's friends and their parents would see the show and, like with my son, I didn't want Rosie to find out about my past from anyone but me. Ten minutes before the show, heart beating against my chest, I called Rosie up to a separate room and told her I needed to tell her something grown-up and important. Her little brown eyes looked surprised and confused as I almost teared up telling her. She was the absolute best and she made it easy for me saying she understood, and that it didn't matter. I've only had a few conversations since then with my kids about my time in prison. Not once have they asked me any more questions, even as my career started to pick up.

My journey to becoming a correspondent on Panorama was an unusual one, to say the least. It all started just after I was released. The campaign for my freedom was earning some real media attention and journalists from everywhere started to jump on the bandwagon. You had the whole range, from rookies trying to make a name for themselves to prominent figures like Kirsty Wark and Jeremy Vine. But then an overlap emerged. I didn't have a clue what to do with my life after I was released. Initially, I only ever intended to use the correspondence course I took in prison to better convince journalists to report about my wrongful conviction. That was my ultimate motive. But now I was free, I was lost. In an act of genius or desperation, probably a mix of both, I started to use my spotlight to my own advantage. I contacted every news journalist who had taken the slightest interest in my story to see if there were opportunities in the business for someone like me. A BBC Radio Five producer agreed to meet me and give me a tour of the studio. Halfway through, we walked through an old television set into an outdoor smoking area. I found myself surrounded by journalists and producers for the country's flagship current affairs news programmes. That's where I met Rod Liddle.

Liddle was the editor of the Today Programme and was always known to be a bit of a maverick. Even then, I was shocked to hear him offer me a job after a single conversation over a cigarette. I'd never even spoken to him before, but he must have taken a liking to me or saw an opportunity. To be fair, that's the kind of guy he was. Still, I couldn't believe my ears. I remember nudging one of the men next to me, Ishmael, who urged me to go for it. Who would turn down the Today Programme? I said that I'd think about it. By the end of my Radio Five Tour, I had managed to secure a different opportunity to do some work experience with BBC London.

The placement lasted four weeks and the editor at the time, a man by the name of Sandy Smith, took me under his wing. For those four weeks, I was stationed next to Emily Maitlis. Back then she was on regional, but you'll know her now as the presenter of Newsnight. She was an incredibly driven woman and was midway through her journey to forge out a name for herself in the industry. Being in that environment gave me a feeling for what it meant to be a journalist. The only semblance of an experience I had in the industry was from the journalists who used to ask me questions back in prison, digging for information about my predicament. It's safe to say I was used to being on the other side of the notepad and the thought of switching terrified me.

The stage fright was justified. Early on into my placement, I was made to go out into the field by myself with no training whatsoever. I barely knew how to use a camera and I had no idea how to use a microphone. I pretended to know what I was doing but it was safe to say that I'd been chucked right into the deep end. You have to remember that, at this point, it had been less than a year since I'd been released.

Everyone around me was frantically chasing a career while I was just trying to enjoy life again and live in the moment, a luxury that had been taken away from me for twelve years. I was still moving at prison pace, and still using prison slang to communicate. There was one moment with Emily which I am sure has stuck with me more than it has with her. After trying to strike up a conversation with her, she responded with a puzzled expression as if to say, "what the hell are you talking about?" I don't think we ever spoke again.

Back then, I was too stuck in that prison mentality. It made sense that the most important thing I was to learn from that placement wasn't anything about journalism or reporting. It was how to reintegrate myself back into society.

All the while, Rod Liddle stayed in contact with me. He picked up the phone, more than once, and insisted that I came to work for him. He refused to take no for an answer. It worked.

"DOING THOSE PROGRAMMES TAUGHT ME THAT SURVIVAL IN HOSTILE ENVIRONMENTS CAME NATURALLY TO ME. IT ALL CAME FROM PRISON."

10

JOINING
THE BBC

Chapter 10

BBC journalist

I'd heard it all about the Today Programme long before I'd joined. It was home to John Humphrys, Jim Naughtie and Sarah Montague as well as other 'who's who' presenters. Though it was far from my favourite programme, I'd even listened to it in prison. What I didn't know was how important it was to the nation. Everyone listened to it, from your movers and shakers to politicians, all the way up to the Prime Minister. It had that influence. My knowledge of this was the reason I chose to arrive on my first day at the BBC Television Centre in a suit, the very suit I wore the day I was released from prison.

In my mind, that's how they would want me to dress. From what I'd seen on television, no one in this business was going to look like me. I was brown-skinned, dreadlocked and four weeks at the BBC had done nothing to my hybrid dialect of prison slang and cockney. To that, add the fact everyone in that office had just seen me walk out of the Court of Appeal with a raised fist declaring that I'd been made to waste twelve years of my life in prison. I was destined to stick out like a sore thumb so there was no way I was going to make it worse.

I walked into the office and what I did see? Jeans. A sea of jeans and scruffy T-shirts and trainers. I stood stiff in the reception area until Rod Liddle came to walk me to his office. His chest was out, evidently proud to be parading around this "young-black-dreadlocked-wrongly-imprisoned-for-twelve-years" man to the staff who gawked at me from behind their desks. Rod gave me the job offer in his office. It was to go out and sit on what they called the planning desk with a man called Jamie. After that, I was given a tour. I met Jim Naughtie and James Naughtie. I met the other presenters and the senior producers of the program. All white. There were no black people. There were no Asian people. There was nobody of colour or any other ethnicity. It was just me. That was already an uncomfortable feeling. And there I was, in a fucking suit.

Over the next three days, I discovered what my job really was. While I sat next to Jamie, I was to pick up the phone and convince politicians or other people of note to come on the program and talk about the topic of the day. The trouble was that politicians didn't want to hear from ordinary people. I sat at that desk for three days bottling up my frustration. I plucked up the courage to go to Rod and explain that I just couldn't do it. I'd signed a three-month contract with the Today Programme, and I appreciated the opportunity, but I couldn't do what he wanted me to do. I felt like I worked at a call-centre. To my surprise, he turned to me and said, "Why don't you go and work as a reporter?"

That was it. Rod pointed out that they didn't have anyone who looked like me or behaved like me. I was thirty-two at the time but twelve years in prison meant I still had all the characteristics of a twenty-year-old. I think he fed off my energy; there was a lot of banter shared between us. Plus, truth be told, Rod fancied himself to be a bit of a street guy. He was fascinated by the criminal underworld and took any chance he could to talk with me about it. He couldn't get over the fact that I knew all these notorious gangsters who he knew no-one could get access to. Apart from me, that is. I'd blow his mind when I'd tell him about the experiences I'd had. Looking back, that was probably one of his key motives for hiring me. But I do think he genuinely enjoyed our conversations. Every day I would come to sit down in a room full of people who were eloquent in a language that was foreign to me. They were educated white people who had gone to Oxford or Cambridge or some other place like that. They all spoke the same, looked the same and behaved in the same way. They oozed this confidence that was just alien to someone like me, not just because of my years in prison, but because of my upbringing. In the face of all of that, it was Rod who told me to be myself. So, I took up his offer to try my hand at reporting.

I got some interesting looks from the other Today reporters. "Who the fuck is he?" "Where did he come from?" I could read it right off their faces. There were a few that were encouraging like Shaun Ley. He is one of the political correspondents who now presents Sunday morning politics programmes. The majority of the reporters were threatened because they knew I was being brought in predominantly to look at crime and criminal justice. They couldn't compete with me at that. They were petrified that in due course I would replace them, and it wasn't just the reporters. Some producers wanted to be where I was, and others had seen that I'd only just been at the reporter's desk. I didn't have any kind of reputation. I'd only found out about Smart-phones a couple of months ago and, all of a sudden, I was being asked to put together a package for the Today Programme with equipment that I'd never seen before. The only thing I had was the gift of the gab. That's the only thing that had convinced Rod that I could do it.

One of the first assignments that Rod and I agreed on was for me to establish a package that looked at whether Reggie Kray believed that his brother, Ronnie, had killed his wife. It was a rumour that had circulated for many years. The fact that I had a relationship with Reggie Kray sealed the deal. I'd even got to know his partner, Bradley, in prison. I went to Spain and tracked down Bradley, who now lives in England, to find out whether Ronnie had ever confessed to the murder of Reggie's wife. I then got busy contacting Leonard Read, known as Nipper Read, the copper who put the Kray twins in prison. Nipper gave me this fantastic interview embellished with content that he'd never shared with anyone before. Finally, I'd done something right. I had to get the forty-five minutes' worth of recordings I'd captured down to a minute and a half, so I thought I'd do it on the train back to the office to save time. I erased the entire thing. One click of a button and the whole recording was gone. Sod's law, if I'd ever seen it. I'd only been taught how to edit mini discs very quickly and I was still a novice with the equipment. The thought of having to go back to the office empty-handed terrified me. I say terrified but, more than anything, I was embarrassed. I'd undermined myself and my ability. This one mishap would give my questioners, enemies, and all the people who said I didn't deserve to be on the Today Programme the ammunition to say, "Rod got it wrong", "Rod shouldn't have employed this guy". I needed a game plan. The second I got to the office, I called Nipper Read and explained what I'd done. After an apology and a bit of grovelling, he agreed to give me another interview there and then over the phone. That saved my skin and opened the door to my next assignment which was to be Afghanistan.

I had only left the country once or twice and now my second assignment was to fly to the most dangerous place in the world to cover a story about heroin.

Those were the kind of once-in-a-lifetime opportunities I was given by being at the BBC.

It's safe to say that the BBC had a profound effect on my career. But it also did its part in helping me heal. There was a bar down the road from the television centre that we would always get the same Pinot Grigio from. I didn't even know what it was at the time and now it's one of my favourite wines. One day, Rod and I sat over a glass and he asked me, "why don't we do an essay?" I had told him all about my experiences in prison and he was convinced that an essay would be a powerful way to note them. He had been a political writer for Tony Blair or someone else who was in government. He said we could do a piece about a particular issue to do with criminal justice and top it with an essay. We ended up writing three. The first was about my release from prison and each essay that followed became deeper and more introspective. Rod could articulate my thoughts with ease, the very thoughts I was trying for the life of me to conceal. I wanted to hide my struggles at this point in my career. It was still less than twelve months away from my release and I hadn't yet grown back the habit of making choices. I was still figuring out how to deal with the psychological and physical challenges that stared me in the face every day whilst not wanting anyone to be aware of them. To me, they were weaknesses that I needed to overcome to protect myself from the outside world and I was desperate not to scupper the three-month contract I had with the BBC. Not because it was a career. I loved the opportunity but not for the prestige of being a journalist. To me, it was a distraction. It numbed the suffering that was going on within me. Rod was the first person to help me express that.

Many people in our office didn't like him. They thought he was a bully. I saw a completely different side to Rod. He was supportive and as we got to know each other better, our relationship strengthened based on two things. One was that he was very much a loner, like me. Although I was in a relationship with Nancy at the time, I was alone in the inner journey that I was on. Rod had his own experience of that. He was the boss of a powerful programme. Everything stopped and started with him. Neither of us had anyone else around who shared the same experiences. The other thing was that he didn't feel he could be himself. He had a South London way about him that he would try to enhance. He would play the brute, the cocky type. I remember one occasion when I stopped him getting arrested after he punched someone clean on the nose at a work celebration drinks event. But that wasn't him. He was a highly intelligent man. I don't know what drove him to try to act like someone else, but both of us found ourselves putting on a front every day that we walked into the office.

The three essays that we wrote together caused quite a stir. As you can imagine, they only amplified the concerns people had about my employment. The Daily Mail and the right-wing press, especially, were questioning the sanity of the editor who employed somebody who'd been in prison for all those years. That was before you took into consideration my history of being "naughty" before I went to prison.

How could the BBC dare employ this individual? More importantly than ruffling some rather stuck up feathers, these essays caused a stir among the audience. People were emotionally drawn to this new reporting style. It triggered interest from broadcasters outside of the BBC. I had offers pouring in, throwing money at me to join them as a reporter. But I was loyal to Rod and Steve Mitchell, Head of News for the BBC at the time. Steve came to me one day to offer an extension of my contract and more money. It wasn't loads of money. It was the basic salary of a BBC employee and probably a fraction of what most people were getting. That didn't mean a thing to me. I'd never earned much for so many years so the fact I was suddenly being offered hundreds and hundreds was neither here nor there. I didn't value money or realise what it could buy me. What mattered was that I was being offered an opportunity to extend my time at the BBC. I'd started my career with hatred being thrown at me from all corners. Now I was being supported and valued.

Greg Dyke, director-general of the BBC, once sent me a message. The Daily Mail had been on their usual ramblings about my being an ex-criminal. But Dyke sent me a note that I keep in my blue treasure box to this day. It read, "don't let the buggers get you down". He went a step further and publicly condemned the corporation as "hideously white" and said its race relations were as bad as those in some police forces. I was a novice reporter for the BBC which had tens of thousands of employees and the director-general had taken the time to send me, this dreadlocked black guy, a note. Dyke earned my respect.

The support grew and I was even invited to meet the then Chair of the BBC, Gavyn Davis, at 7.30a.m. I walked into his office without a clue as to why someone like him would want to meet someone like me. But there was a fascination with my experiences. Like Rod, people had this child-like curiosity about how I could have survived what I came through. Gavyn and I met over tea and scones which were far from the porridge or fry-up I grew up having in the morning. To me, Gavyn, a former economist, was a wealthy elite man of a different calibre. But as we spoke the veil of his privilege began to drop and we found we had a very personal thing in common. He spoke about having sons and how hard it can be to build a relationship with your boys. I hadn't seen my son in years, and I believe Gavyn had an estranged relationship with his. My experience with Gavyn stood for much more than a pleasant chat over breakfast. It marked that even the most senior people were on my side. I realised that if I had support at that level, or at least perceived support, I was going to be okay, no matter what people said about me. I buckled down and I learned my craft. That stint as a reporter on the Today Programme led to my role on the BBC's six o'clock news.

Jay Hunt, now creative director at Apple, was the editor of the six o'clock news. There had been a high-profile stabbing in Peckham that she wanted me to cover. My guess was either they didn't have any black reporters or the few that they had they didn't feel they could put on the street. Neither applied to me, so they probably assumed I was equipped to do the story. The reason didn't matter to me. It was an opportunity and a prestigious one at that. The whole experience changed me. I worked with Nikita Fargo, and cameraman Tony Fallshaw whilst I continued my day job at the Today Programme. I got a flavour for television and became a special investigative reporter for the six o'clock news. I'd started to make a reputation for myself. The BBC was about to launch BBC Three, a channel dedicated to a young British audience. I was approached to become one of their main current affairs investigative journalists.

For the next three years on the Today Programme, I worked for the six o'clock news and as an undercover journalist for the new BBC Three platform. I started work on the "This World" programme for the BBC and worked for BBC Two. My career at the BBC had become stable. I was confident and a lot of the criticism I had received in the early stages of my career had long disappeared. It would pop up now and then, but I would always steer the conversation from who I was back to the stories I was doing. I was in control of my narrative.

You might have wondered how I wound up in Afganistan. On September 11, 2001, the Twin Towers had been brought down in the USA. In the UK, the Labour Government were about to stand shoulder to shoulder with the American Government with the imminent prospect of being dragged into a war. To say it was a tense time would be an understatement.

Jack Straw, Foreign Secretary at the time, had been claiming that one of the main reasons the government used to justify the war in Afghanistan was that the country supplied 85% of the heroin that came into the UK. If the government decided to go to war in Afghanistan, it would be to eradicate the poppy fields and destroy this source of income that was helping to fund terrorism.

This was back when I was working at the Today Programme for BBC Radio. I was a rookie journalist and was watching this huge story unfold around the world. Osama Bin Laden and Al Qaeda were plastered across the newspaper headlines every single day. The Today Programme asked me to go to Afghanistan.

My mission was to journey there with a producer and travel the same journey that the heroin would travel from Afghanistan back to Britain.

We jetted off on this none-too-safe journey with bags packed and bellies full of excitement. We travelled via Islamabad where we had a stopover. The culture shock became very real. I looked every inch the western journalist and still had my dreadlocks. Not quite the same look as the locals. I remember coming out of our hotel for a walk to the shops and hearing the call to prayer. Having never heard it before, my head ticked round to try and find where it was coming from. It just seemed to come out of the sky.

The following day, we went to the airport to meet with our hosts: the United Nations Drugs Programme – the UNDP. I looked at the planes waiting at the gates, wondering which one of those big metal birds was going to take us to our next destination. None of them did. We were to travel in a tiny ten-seater single-propeller plane that meant we could fly low without being detected. This was starting to sound dangerous.

I never wanted to be a war reporter. In fact, I especially wanted not to be a war reporter. But here I found myself in a real warzone that made Brixton Prison look like a safer option!

As we started to approach our destination, we were warned by the pilot that, to avoid any missiles that might be coming in, we might have to fly even lower and make sudden turns, but that this was not a cause for concern. Without any more notice, not even a "cabin crew take your seats, please", we dropped like a stone. At one point the plane was almost upside down. We span back the right way up only to begin climbing the mountains at such a low altitude the plane was bumped all over the place. I could've jumped out of my skin.

We landed in Afghanistan in a patch of desert. I'll admit that I was completely oblivious to the dangers we were in. Probably just as well. We landed to find a group of people there to meet the plane, all westerners. Though there was a convoy of vehicles for our fellow passengers, ours never showed up. My producer and I were left to wait alone with just the representative of the UNDP and the pilot. And a hell of a lot of sand. A fair bit of time passed before the United Nations team turned up with some less than encouraging news. The accommodation that we were supposed to stay in at the UN base had been the target of an attack and had been blown up the day before. They announced that the best they could offer us was a brick shed with a hammock and a mosquito net inside. This would be our home for the next few days.

This was the first time travelling that I really had to rough it. Even my cell back home was more comfortable, and it didn't have the sound of cockroaches and creepy-crawlies wandering about during the night. I tucked in everything I could, but they still found a way in. I slept as stiff as a mummy with one eye open all night! In the morning, I'd get up in the broad daylight and shiver off anything that had wormed its way onto me overnight. I'd have to build myself up to sleep in there every time that night fell.

One of the first journeys we went on took us out into the poppy fields in the heart of a mountainous desert area. It was surreal; we were in the middle of nowhere surrounded by acres upon acres of poppy fields as far as the eye could see. This was where the heroin was coming from. We drove down a track and came across a small wooden kiosk by the side of the road. At first glance, you would have expected it to be selling coffee. Instead, they were selling poppy paste, which was turning many Afghans into addicts. The one guy that manned it kept a firm grip on an AK47 rifle.

The following day, after fighting off the bugs once again, we were due to meet a drug lord. My producer had fallen victim to Delhi Belly and wasn't going anywhere that was further than six feet from a toilet. I would have to travel to meet the drug lord on my own. The journey would see me travel from the middle of Afghanistan up to the north. The war itself was in Kabul, a day and a half away by road, but that didn't minimise the danger I was in.

So it was that I ended up sitting down in front of a warlord who controlled all the acres of heroin that stretched out before us. He was surrounded by barrages of men, all clutching onto AK47 guns. Make no mistake, it wasn't to protect him from me or even from the Americans that patrolled the area. Those guns were his deterrent from the other drug lords who wanted to take over his business. To me, he was quite amiable. He shared with me why they did what they did and how they did it, which I would later weave into a gripping radio piece about heroin.

The next leg of my journey took me to Turkey, or more specifically, down to the Bosporus Strait, which is where the heroin crossed from Afghanistan into Turkish borders. The police allowed me to shadow their raids on known heroin dealers and to see the suitcases full of heroin they'd seized at the airport. I then followed the heroin into the UK. It had found its way into the hands of a young girl in Southend, a user who injected into her arm that very pure heroin fresh in from Afghanistan.

The purpose of the story was to demonstrate just how far removed the users, like the girl from Southend, were from where their heroin had been manufactured. We'd headed straight into the jaws of danger to showcase the importance of damming the drug's pipeline into UK shores. Not bad for my first foreign story for the BBC, if I do say so myself.

Before I could unpack my bags, BBC Three asked me to do another foreign story. This time it was about blood diamonds and it was to be for television rather than radio. Conflict diamonds were receiving more and more attention as designers like Alexander McQueen began featuring them extensively in their collections. At the time Miss Dynamite, a UK rapper, had just released a very powerful song about it. This issue wasn't going to bed anytime soon.

I was in touch with Global Witness, an organization who happened to do a lot of work around conflict diamonds. It was then decided that I would go undercover and travel to Sierra Leone to see if I could source some diamonds. The European Union had drawn up something called the Kimberley Process. This was a certification process which all diamond dealers anywhere in the world would have to follow to ensure that diamonds came from legitimate sources and not from conflict zones. In my opinion, the process was flawed and, in turn, vulnerable to abuse.

Another objective of the investigation was to see if there were any links between terrorism and the diamonds. The Americans had drawn up their most-wanted list on a pack of cards. The first card was Osama Bin Laden and all the others had the names and faces of other terrorists around the world who were wanted for attacks like the Nairobi bombings, or the American bombings.

These were events that had taken a lot of people's lives and the Americans needed answers. With our task made crystal clear, I formed a team with Rachel, a self-filming producer, and a former city police officer who specialised in diamonds. The three of us travelled to Sierra Leone.

This was a little different to Afghanistan. I had to go undercover and my character had to be watertight. I decided to take on the persona of a diamond dealer who was going out to Sierra Leone to purchase diamonds to bring back to Hatton Garden in London. The policeman stayed close by my side as a specialist, keeping his eyes peeled to inspect the diamonds.

The area we first entered was full of diamond artists and mines. The mines weren't that deep. They were open and there were crowds of men stooped down to wash the stones in water. I found one of the artists and showed both them and the miners the pictures we had of the most wanted terrorists. We got a positive response. Immediately, they started to pick out a number of these terrorists as diamond buyers.

At the time, I didn't realise the significance of what I had discovered. All I knew was that it suggested that these terrorists had moved from heroin to diamonds. They smuggled the gems across borders because they were far less hassle to transport compared to cash or drugs. But now I had witnesses to identify the individuals involved, the story was beginning to take shape. I felt powerful. The work I was doing was making a difference and brought something more to the table than lunchtime entertainment.

Our work was far from done. In order to expose the process, we needed to buy the diamonds, bring them back to England and show that we could sell them. I continued to pose as a buyer, and we managed to secure the help of a local fixer. Our team of three became four. To get the story, our next step was to drive a distance to another area. Out of nowhere, we came up against a checkpoint. This wasn't an official one. It was manned by an unofficial militia group with young boy soldiers who were carrying some very serious looking guns. They stopped us.

We had been trained for this sort of eventuality before we left England when the BBC put us through their hostile environment course. Our training included being shot at with real ammunition. Not only did it help us learn what to expect but it taught us how to recognise the type of ammunition used against us. They also subjected us to a very realistic kidnapping which, to this day, I have not forgiven them for.

All the training in the world counts for nothing when you're staring down the barrel of a gun. The soldiers were speaking French of which I didn't understand a word. They demanded in gestures that Rachel, my camerawoman, get out of the vehicle and go with them into their hut. I thought they were going to rape her. Fight or flight kicked in and I jumped out of the car and followed her. I couldn't tell you how but through some miracle I managed to talk the soldier down into letting her go. They did, and we were lucky; that experience could have easily gone the other way.

We had no time to recover, we had to drive on. Our fixer took us to a camp in Freetown, the capital of Sierra Leone. This camp was the home of amputees and lots of them. During the Civil War, many civilians had their arms, legs and fingers chopped off by militia as a warning. It sent the message that if you didn't hand over the diamonds that you find, you or your relatives will have your limbs chopped off. It served its purpose. The camp was filled with hundreds of children and adults. I'd never seen such a heart-breaking scene in my life. Exposing the conflict diamond trade was a very sensitive issue, and it had become my duty to find out more.

The guy in charge of the camp we called Captain Hook because he'd replaced his two chopped off hands with metal hooks. He was the one who gave us permission to film, but we didn't trust him. Everyone in the camp was living in poverty but he, somehow, seemed to be living a very comfortable life.

We offered to buy some rice for the people in the camp as a gesture of gratitude for letting us share their story. Captain Hook insisted, "Don't give it to the people, give it to me and I'll store and distribute it." It wasn't a surprise to find out later on that he didn't distribute a thing that came through the camp. He kept it all for himself. It was then that I made a mistake. I suppose I thought I was doing the right thing, but I sent our fixer off to buy some rice and to give it straight to the people but not to the boss.

We started to film and interview the people there whilst the fixer distributed some rice. Captain Hook must have caught wind of the news that we didn't plan on following his orders. We were elbow-deep in filming when he called out his soldiers to attack. All of a sudden, we noticed a commotion behind us. A frenzied crowd of people began hopping, crawling and running at a pace even though they didn't have the feet or legs to do it, all heading in one direction. Despite not knowing what was going on, instinct kicked in and we headed in the same direction. To our horror, our fixer was being almost beaten to death by the amputees. Those that didn't have hands were hitting him with their stumps.

I managed to get to him, push the people off and grab him. Our vehicle backed up into the crowd and nudged its way through without hurting them. I was able to lift the fixer up by myself and put him onto the back of our pickup truck. We all scrambled on board and made for the exit.

As we managed to drive out of the camp, they were rocking the vehicle. We didn't know if we were going to make it. The vehicle shook off the last of Captain Hook's soldiers before driving out of the camp and making it halfway down the road. The rest of us were lucky not to have been attacked, but our fixer was in a very bad shape, so we drove straight to the nearest hospital. He was seriously injured but thankfully he didn't die.

Once he'd recovered, we left that region of Freetown and went to another area where I was going to buy diamonds. I resumed my undercover persona. We booked into a hotel. Well, that's what they called it. It was disgusting. If I had dug a hole in the ground, it would have been cleaner than our room. There was blood on the sheets, blood on the floor and blood on the walls. It was like staying in a crime scene.

The undercover police officer and I were waiting to be collected when a western white guy approached where we were standing. You could see in his face that he recognised the undercover guy that I was with. In turn, the policeman also recognised him. We were in the middle of nowhere in Sierra Leone, what were the chances of meeting anyone you knew? Questions I couldn't yet ask flooded my mind. "How did he know him?" "What was the connection here?" Turns out, that man was a known paedophile. Horrible as it was, it was the least of my worries.

Our vehicle arrived to take us off to a secret location to meet the local Mr Big in the black-market diamond trade. Word had got out that one man on Interpol's most wanted criminals list was hiding out in a hotel in Beirut. He was a Lebanese dealer in arms, drugs and diamonds from Sierra Leone. After making contact he agreed to record an interview with me. What he didn't know is that I'd be secretly filming him.

I was wired up with a tiny camera hidden on my shirt. It'd have to be a shirt with buttons in the front so the camera could be easily disguised as one. Those cameras were completely invisible, but when you wear one you can't help but feel super aware of it. Covert filming isn't easy. There's a lot of technique that goes into it. If you are not careful, you can make the rookie mistake of tilting the camera up to the ceiling, missing all of the action. Before that you had the challenge of getting dressed with the thing, running the wires and connecting everything up. The only way is to do it in front of a mirror. A wire would run down inside my clothes and into a recording box with a memory card. Over the years, this equipment would become smaller and smaller and more sophisticated. We weren't there yet. While I was filming in Beirut, there was always a lump sticking out of me somewhere. But I was good at this job. I was so good at what I did no-one suspected me, or maybe that's because I was black with dreadlocks. Either way, nerves of steel were required for this kind of reporting so much so that in the moment, it is easy to forget to press the record button.

There was always the risk that someone would look at my shirt buttons and see that there was one button that didn't have the bit of cotton that every other button had. It just had two black holes, very small black holes, which is where the cameras were. If somebody was looking at it, I would always know. For many years after that, I was always looking at people's buttons to make sure they weren't trying to secretly record conversations with me. Why they would, I don't know.

In Beirut, the Lebanese dealer calmly sat there as he admitted to me that he smuggled a million pounds worth of diamonds every week and traded them in the open market. He was extremely wealthy and very blunt about what he did. It was bizarre. There he was boasting, looking all threatening and dangerous while I secretly recorded him. However, that was my life as an undercover journalist.

To smuggle diamonds is a very dangerous business as we had discovered in the amputee's camp. The rewards, however, seemed to outweigh the risk for many of the locals who would try and earn a little extra income. They certainly needed it. I needed it to make my story.

The big man arrived and was sitting at a table in front of us which was covered with stones. He showed off the different sizes and qualities and offered them for us to buy. The diamonds didn't look like what I thought a diamond looked like. In the UK, I'd only seen the polished little geometric ones, the kind that prodded out of rings or necklaces. What I saw here was miles away from that. I'm talking about hundreds of thousands of little black stones that haven't been polished or cleaned or cut. They just looked like lumps of black charcoal.

There was a knock on the door and the big man let them in. These rough-looking guys scuffled in with little black bags and put them on the table. He would give them a handful of cash and they would leave. He was trying to persuade me to buy a larger quantity of stones, but I insisted that I just needed to take some samples to my guys in Hatton Garden for them to evaluate.

If they liked them, I would be back for more. Things were starting to get a bit heated because the big man insisted that I buy more. He wanted me to give him more money. My undercover police officer started to get scared and it showed. He was trying to pick up the diamonds but his hands shook like a leaf. He was shaken and it irritated me.

This was very real, and it always had the potential to get dangerous. Not once did I let my persona drop. I couldn't. Neither of us could! This guy was a criminal surrounded by criminals all armed with guns I'm sure they weren't scared to use. They would have our guts for garters if we roused even the slightest suspicion. In the end, I bought a few hundred dollars' worth of black diamonds and told him I'd be back. It was touch and go but we managed to get out safely with the diamonds. Had they found the camera that I was wearing, we wouldn't have made it out of there alive. That was the kind of risk that I'd taken.

We left the big man and his men to go back to our blood-stained 'executive suite' for the debrief and to check our footage.

Later that evening, I was sitting in my room and I heard knocking on the door. I was greeted by three guys speaking in either Afrikaans or French. Whatever it was, I couldn't understand them. They seemed to know that I was a diamond buyer and had money. Word travels fast. They were insisting that I buy their diamonds. In fact, it was a bit more than insisting. They bordered on threatening.

They could have robbed me there and then, but I was able to persuade them to come back later. Their impromptu visit was enough to tell me we had to get out of there. I contacted the rest of my team, told them what happened, and we all agreed that our lives were in danger. We packed up, ran downstairs and jumped straight into our vehicle to drive off.

It wasn't long before we noticed that we were being followed. Our quick and quiet escape transformed into a full-blown car chase as we sped down the dirt road to the helipad. It was our only way out. We had no idea who it was that was following us but if they were anything like the new friends I'd made at our hotel, we did not want to find out. By the skin of our teeth, we were able to outrun them and beat them to the helipad. The only helicopter available was a Russian one so old it would not have looked out of place in a museum.

Beggars can't be choosers. We hired it and escaped out of Freetown with our footage, diamonds and lives intact.

When the helicopter landed, I recorded a piece to camera on the bridge. This was my first television documentary, so I was still getting used to this new format. Radio had been a lot easier. But, ever skilled, my producer Rachel helped me record some great material.

It wasn't until we arrived back that the enormity of what we had just experienced began to sink it. For the first time, I started to think of just how many times in the last few days my life had been in danger. The following day the crew and I decided to take some well-earned relaxation time and drive to a beach. Its beauty was unbelievable and there was not a soul there except us. It was exactly what we needed after such a traumatic time.

We returned home to complete the last part of the assignment. We had to prove how easy it was to bring in and sell blood diamonds here. I'd already managed to smuggle the diamonds back to England and, to this day, I've never revealed where I concealed them or how I did it. We put back on the covert filming gear and I went on my own to Hatton Garden to meet with the diamond dealers. With all the publicity and awareness about blood diamonds and the circumstances surrounding them, by now nobody should have been buying diamonds from street dealers like me. I quickly found that this was not the case.

Every shop that I walked into I would drop the stones on the counter. The dealer would pick a stone up, look at it with their eyeglass and then offer me money. I would tell them that I had no certification for the stones, but they replied that it didn't matter. There you had it. The whole premise of the programme was to show that the Kimberley Process did not work. Dealers didn't care about it, all they cared about was making money. That moment made clear that the process introduced to protect people suffering in conflict zones, like those who had lost their limbs in Sierra Leone, was pointless. As far as the programme was concerned, it was mission accomplished. We made the documentary and when it went out, it caused quite the stir. Job done.

After the programme aired, I remember taking those diamonds into the office and giving them to the production manager who put them in a drawer. No one would've guessed what those black stones were. Years and years later, I got contacted by the police asking me if I still had the diamonds that they'd seen on the documentary. As the first to expose its flaws, the programme had become a reference point for the Kimberley Process to the authorities. The police hounded me for the location, and I gave them the only answer I could, that my production manager put them in a drawer in the office. By then the office was long gone; the BBC had moved from the old Television Centre in Shepherd's Bush.

Those diamonds have never been found and I have no idea what happened to them. I'm sure the police were convinced that I had one polished and used it as an engagement ring, but I hadn't.

Funny though, I would have saved myself a few quid if I had! I was proud of what we achieved with the programme. Not only was it my first documentary, but it took me into parts of the world that I knew very little about. The fear and danger were overcome by the excitement I felt to be enjoying the freedom to travel, a freedom I'd not had for twelve years.

Doing those programmes taught me that survival in hostile environments came naturally to me. It all came from prison. There I thought that my twelve years gave me nothing to draw on for this new career. As fate would have it, the abilities I developed from reading people and dealing with situations in prison taught me how to take on a persona, to 'duck and dive' if you like and to manoeuvre through the challenges I faced on the job. These skills were to take me through places where even the police feared to tread.

On another occasion, I went undercover for the BBC as a doorman in Manchester. The idea was to expose the fact that there were a lot of drugs flowing through nightclubs up there. How were they getting them in? The thinking was that whoever controlled the doors, controlled the drugs. Were the firms that employed doormen responsible for the drug flow of cocaine and ecstasy inside clubs? We went in to find out.

I was introduced to someone already working in the nightclub scene as a doorman. He was also undercover and had gathered some prima facia evidence that suggested our hypothesis was right. He became my handler. He instructed me to go to Manchester, change my name, book into a cheap hotel. I was to stay low-key at all costs. After a few days, I went in search of work with a reference from a guy I'd met up there. He'd embedded himself in this scene and had built up a reputation. There were plenty of security companies supplying doormen and stewards and there was no shortage of work.

He introduced me and told them I had been in prison. In that world, it was an advantage.

Every day in my hotel, I'd wire myself up with my covert camera kit and be put to work on the doors of pubs and clubs all over the city. I hated it! On any one night, there would be drunks, fights and attacks or all three. I had to wear a stab vest for my protection. As time went on, I integrated myself into the scene and was acquitting myself well. It wasn't long before I was introduced to the main man and managed to get into a trusted position. It was there that I learned about the illegal drug trade as well as the illegal extortion. Not without risk.

I was an undercover reporter using a false name. The only people who knew this were my handler, who was my fellow BBC employee, and the guy who gave me the original introduction. I was very aware of the danger of being exposed so, after my shift as a doorman, I would always take a roundabout way of going home to lose anybody who might have been following me. One evening, having made this convoluted journey I arrived back at my hotel and the reception called me over to say that they had an envelope for me. I thought it must be from my handler. I took the envelope and written on it was my real name, Mr Rowe.

My stomach dropped. I was undercover! No one knew my surname, which meant that something was very wrong. Still hoping it could be from the BBC, I opened it. Inside were two Football tickets to the Manchester United v Arsenal football match at Old Trafford that weekend. Who could have sent them? Had my cover been blown? Was this a setup? If I went, would my life be in danger? When you're undercover being paranoid is a part of the job. It's how you stay alive.

I wondered if they had been sent by my friend Pat Younge, Head of Sport for the BBC, but then he had nothing to do with what I was doing here, and wouldn't have known where I was.

Could the tickets be from my handler, as a reward? Perhaps he wanted to give me a chance to blow off some steam and take a break from the intensity of being an undercover. I'd been undercover for two months already, and it had been difficult. But when I called my handler to say thanks, he asked what for. He knew nothing about the tickets. If they hadn't been going off before, alarm bells started to rattle my brain. Was I being set up?

Anyone who knew me well enough to know I was a football fan, would've simply identified themselves. If I had indeed been exposed, the best place to get at me was in a crowded space such as a football stadium, where there would be hundreds of thousands of football fans and an 'accident' might occur. The only trouble was... that I wanted to go.

I came up with a plan that meant I could both see the game and figure out if I had a target on my back. I called a friend who lived in Manchester and explained to him that I had two tickets to go to this game, but that I thought it could be a setup. He agreed to come with me. We drove to Old Trafford and parked the car. I looked around to see if I was being followed (I'm good at surveillance) and we went into the stadium, but there was nothing out of the ordinary. The seats were great. So was the game. But I kept watching out of the corner of my eye, for anything that stood out or seemed off. Nothing did.

Ten minutes before the end of the game, I nudged my friend and said to him, "If we leave now and we're followed out, then I'll know that I've been exposed, and who's set me up."

So we got up. We left and we reached the car park safely. We got into the car and drove off. As far as we could tell, nobody followed us. I dropped my friend off and followed a circuitous route before entering the hotel. Nobody has come forward to identify themselves as my phantom benefactor. I've asked many people over the years, but to this day I still don't know who sent me the tickets. Maybe I never will.

Looking back at my undercover days, no one had ever done what I was doing at the BBC. This was a first. I was breaking new ground with every assignment, and I was doing it in a way that made my colleagues' jaws drop. No one had put their life in as much danger as I had to get a story or to make a TV programme.

Had my cover been blown in any of those cases, I'd have been dead. When I was out in the field, there was no protection, no minders and no escape route. When I sat down with those warlords in Afghanistan, for example, I didn't realise just how much danger I was putting myself in. It wasn't just the people who were dangerous, it was also the terrain. We were once driving in a convoy of two UN vehicles, along a narrow mountain track carved into the side of a cliff, when one of the vehicles broke down and ended up hanging over the edge of the cliff. There was nothing we could do. There is no AA to come to the rescue in Afghanistan. We ended up spending the night in the vehicles and having to dig ourselves out of the problem the following morning.

On our stop, I picked up a spent shell from an AK47. I brought it back to the BBC as a souvenir for Rod, just to remind him that there is a real-world out there, one that you can't see from behind a desk.

We started doing a series called the Underworld Rich List. It was for BBC Two and BBC Three and was to be a three-part series looking into the richest criminals, fraudsters and smugglers.

One of the richest smugglers in the United Kingdom was a guy called Tom Slab Murphy. At the time, he was a commanding officer for the Irish Republican Army, the IRA. He had a farm in County Armagh and County Louth, straddling the border between Northern Ireland and the Republic of Ireland – right on the Larkins Road. That road happens to be the only one in Europe where oil tankers have been banned from travelling along, as a result of oil smuggling between the two countries.

Murphy was thought to be smuggling oil through tunnels and tubes under his farm. His unit was also thought to be responsible for the death of more British soldiers during the conflict in Ireland, than any other unit in the IRA.

That's why we went to go and film his farm. A crew and I flew to Ireland to capture the story. There were four of us – a producer Fatima, who's now been promoted to commissioning editor, a cameraman Dave Langton, a security guard and me.

We arrived in the area along Larkins road, in a vehicle with blacked-out windows. The only way we could film was to cruise very, very slowly past the farm, holding a camera to the window. As we filmed the yard, we spotted an oil tanker. Then that oil tanker spotted us. A group of men in balaclavas jumped into two Range Rovers and drove after us. No time for chitchat, or to ask them what they wanted; we slammed the accelerator.

My driver, who I had thought to be just a private security guard, suddenly pulled out a gun from his jacket and put it on his lap. I found myself in yet another high-speed car chase, that would have done a Hollywood film justice. Fatima was terrified in the back seat, and my cameraman, while trying to film out the back, dropped his camera. It was a desperate situation. I picked up the phone and punched in the numbers to call the production office in London.

"We are in a high-speed car chase on the Larkins Road being pursued by the IRA, who may have guns." They didn't ask if we were okay or if we were going to make it. She only had one question.

"Are you filming it?" she replied.

We were up to our necks in danger. Then the driver veered off the road and cut across a field to join the main road. We drove through some barriers, and then into the back yard of the Garda Station, a remote police station, and as we pulled in, the two Range Rover vehicles pulled up slowly outside. They observed us for a moment, and just when we thought it was all over for us, they drove off. It was a very narrow escape. Had they realised that we were a film crew for the BBC and that we had a member of the constabulary on board, it could have ended very differently. Frankly, I had felt safer in Sierra Leone.

I had been chiselling away on these other programs until 2006 when I was asked by the Today Programme to make a decision. Either I had to dedicate my career to the Today Program, or I had to leave and turn my attention towards the other platforms I'd been working on. It just so happened that at this time I had been investigating the murder of Jill Dando, the BBC presenter. She had been assassinated on her doorstep, and a man by the name of Barry George had been arrested and convicted. His sister, however, had approached me to look into it. At this point in my career, I was thinking about expanding my repertoire of stories. I had done one or two around miscarriages of justice, but I did not want that to become my only forte. The conviction of Barry George bothered me because there was something wrong about how it had been reported. It reminded me of how the journalists had reported my case: you could tell from their words, that they knew something was wrong, but nothing was being done. I took up the Barry George case in my own time. I didn't have much support from within the BBC.

After all, Jill Dando was one of their own and you can't investigate the murder of one of your own presenters. I came up against a lot of opposition among senior commissioners and editors at the BBC, but I'd managed to gain the support of Karen O'Connor, head of the BBC's current affairs, and Mike Lewis, who was up in the Manchester office. I started to find the story by doing what I do best: pounding the pavement. I knocked on people's doors and invited them to talk to me openly and honestly about what they saw, or what they didn't see. I looked through police documentation, not for what could be seen at face value, but for inconsistencies or discrepancies. Muscle memory kicked in from all the years I'd been doing that with my own documents.

My gut instinct had been right, and it became glaringly obvious to me that something in the Jill Dando/ Barry George case was seriously wrong. Word got out. People knew that I had been investigating the case for about eighteen months, and had come up with new information and I think that people were embarrassed about the fact that they weren't doing what I was doing. Both the BBC current affairs department and Panorama wanted it commissioned. Mike Robinson, editor of Panorama at the time, offered me an hour slot for it. Everyone said I had to give it to Panorama. They were such a great platform. But I didn't see why I should. They hadn't wanted it in the first place. Why would we give it to them now, now that we'd done all the hard work?

After a while, even the proudest parts of myself couldn't deny how big a deal Panorama was. That one-hour segment played out at primetime on BBC Panorama and attracted the biggest current affairs audience the programme had had for a very long time. It was hugely controversial. How dare the BBC undermine the conviction of the man that had killed one of their own? But it was a success, in that the evidence I presented and the way I'd gone about investigating the case, was different from any reporter before me. Many would deem the way that I interviewed members of the jury illegal, but all I did was present information and evidence that was not in front of them at the time they convicted Barry George – and then asked a very simple question: had you known back then what I am showing you now, would you have reached the same conclusion? Unequivocally, the answer came back no. I even asked the foreman of the jury, who was outraged that what I presented was not shown during the trial. No one had ever done that before. That's what helped make the show the success it was.

Soon after, Sandy Smith was appointed as the new editor of Panorama. During that time, Panorama underwent a rebirth. It had been dug out of its Sunday graveyard slot to primetime on Monday nights at 8.30p.m. for a half-hour show. Jeremy Vine became the host. I had been instrumental to Panorama's shift because it was my investigation into Barry George that had gotten the show noticed again. This was confirmed to me when Sandy Smith approached me, and another outside journalist John Sweeney, to be the new reporters for the show. Like me, John Sweeney was also a maverick journalist. He'd been a former correspondent for the Observer and had covered Scientology as well as other left-field stories. This was to be another turning point. That's just what I did at the BBC. Even before this, throughout my whole career at the BBC – I made history. I was the only person of colour, with dreadlocks, to come from a background like mine, having spent twelve years in prison for a crime I did not commit, to work on these prestigious programmes. Now Panorama. No one had ever done what I did, and no one has since. I proved that, with the right will and skills, everything is possible.

In 2006, I stepped away from the Today Programme and the six o'clock news, to dedicate myself fully to Panorama. In just eight years, I was being offered a correspondent position. This time I had more confidence walking into a new office because now I had a reputation. People knew my work. But despite that, I was still a box-ticker. With no Asian or Black staff, people still wanted to work with me for my brown skin, dreadlocks, and 'urban' accent. My prison slang had been diluted with BBC language to a certain degree, but I still had my own twang. My voice had become just as distinctive on television, as it had been on the radio. But no matter how much popularity it drew, I always knew I was never accepted amongst everyone. I just wasn't one of them, and I wasn't like them. It didn't bother me, which said a lot. I'd seen many come and go who could not withstand the embedded racism and discrimination within the BBC.

Sandy Smith remained a mentor and believed in bringing in people like me to offer change and do things differently. He gave me free creative reign which meant that 99.9% of every program that I ever made at Panorama was my idea. Quite unlike my white counterparts who, in all the years I was at the programme, only came to me twice with an idea for a programme. But the BBC still treated me like an outsider, even though I was a correspondent at the top of my game. Panorama was a depressing, unfriendly place to work in the best of times; everyone was buried in deep investigations. That said, I did manage to make my mark with some powerful documentaries which exposed domestic and international issues of importance.

As a victim of knife crime, and a carrier of a knife in my teenage years, I was keen to make a film about knife crime. I hoped that it would deter young people from carrying knives. Those blades raised the risk of them being a victim of knife crime, or a perpetrator of one, that for many led to a murder charge. 'Jailed for Knife', was a Panorama exclusive where I met and interviewed convicted teenagers serving long prison sentences for using or carrying a knife.

The radicalisation of prisoners by Islamic extremists in UK prisons was another powerful, real and current insight into the challenges the British government faced, that we brought to air. I conducted a number of dangerous international investigations for Panorama. Some were highly rewarding, not financially or through recognition, but personally.

On one occasion, I even rescued a chained Orangutan from a river community in Sumatra, Indonesia. I was investigating deforestation connected with palm oil production led by some mighty corporates, supplying even mightier western corporates, who mislead the public about their social responsibilities by not sourcing from sustainable companies.

After capturing the deforestation on film, I was on my way back with my crew, going down the river to safe ground, when I spotted a small orangutan sitting on the edge of a wooden platform. A chain was clamped around its neck which fastened the animal to a wooden pole. We stopped, and I spoke to the river people living on the bank. They told me that its parents had been killed when city companies cleared the forest for palm oil. That little orangutan was brought to the village as a tiny baby by one of the labourers and had been living with them in chains for about 5 years. I was shocked and saddened by the sight. He was underfed and dirty but was an amazing animal. I pleaded with the villagers, and with luck they allowed us to rescue him. A few days later we managed to get him placed in a rescue camp, where they welcomed him and committed to caring for him. Just before we left, I returned to see how my orangutan friend was holding up. He recognised me and as I stood before him, he slipped a leather bangle from my wrist. My son had given me that bangle. What a story I now had when it came time to tell him where it'd gone.

Environmental stories became a bit of a speciality for me as I went on to investigate illegal logging in the Democratic Republic of Congo. For the programme, we monitored the entire journey of illegal trees, from when they were first chopped down in the jungle, to the products made from them in Europe. It was a difficult and dangerous journey but again, it was one that had never been accomplished before.

Another issue we covered, was the dumping of old electrical parts and appliances in the third world. We were convinced that licensed traders were not properly disposing of these items and simply dumping them overseas. We set out a plan to catch them. I set up a fake shop in London to attract white goods and televisions for recycling. I would plant GPS trackers in these broken items and then contact recycling companies who had declared compliance with The Waste Electric and Electronic Equipment Regulations. In theory, this meant they were committed to disposing of them in a safe and environmentally friendly way. That was far from what was actually happening, and I was determined to prove it. My tracked dodgy goods ended up in shipping containers. One of these was destined to leave the UK when customs stopped it on my tip-off. Two of the others weren't quite as lucky. The GPS trackers showed the approximate location of the electronic waste that had been illegally shipped to different countries in Africa. One container made it to Ghana, and another ended up in Nigeria. I packed my bags and I travelled there with a GPS detection wand to locate them and gather the evidence we needed.

I arrived in Ghana looking like Buzz Lightyear with this glowing little device in my hand. I followed the signal to a remote village. I asked around to see if they knew of anyone who had recently brought a TV into the village. People were obviously suspicious at first, so I told them I had planted a tracker in a television back in England. The person who ended up with it had won a prize of $50. This immediately attracted a lot of interest and before I knew it, I had an entourage of people following me through the village, as it was being filmed by my cameraman and producer, Howard Bradburn. All of a sudden, a young guy approached and said he knew who had the TV and that I should follow him. So we did. He pointed to a door and said, "It's inside there".

I was apprehensive but knocked on the door. I knocked again. Everyone waited in silence before the door opened. Standing there was a huge, bald man wearing boxer shorts. He was rubbing sleep from his eyes and was growling slightly, bemused by the attention. I told him that I was from the UK, and showed him a photo of the TV I was hunting. He denied having a TV. I told him the bleep on the tracking device was going crazy because the signal was close by. He told me that he had recently purchased a TV, but that it did not work. I asked if it was inside and he said no, but then changed his tune. He told me to wait a moment and went inside, only to re-emerge with a black box in hand. It was the tracker. I lied and told him that he had won the prize of $50, but that I needed the TV before I could hand the money over. He said that he'd had it, but when it did not work, he'd opened it up and found the tracker. I then turned to the camera and did a revealingly awkward piece, looking straight down the lens, declaring that our investigation had been successful. But that wasn't the end of the story. Almost as soon as I had landed back in the UK, another tracker placed in a separate TV bleeped from Nigeria. I was able to track it down and return that appliance back to the UK.

You might think that that was too far to go for a busted TV, but electronic waste contains hazardous components that may poison land and people. That is why it is illegal. And what I did, had a positive effect on how the UK Environmental Agency currently polices the industry.

How the world polices itself was my next target. Mission Impossible, like the Tom Cruise film, happened to also be the title of my Panorama investigation into UN Peacekeepers rearming militia rebels in the Congo. In exchange for gold, Peacekeepers were providing weapons to rebel soldiers who were known for barbaric acts of cannibalism and savage killings of innocent civilians.

The investigation stretched across three continents: Europe, America and one of the most dangerous places in the world, the Democratic Republic of Congo, in Africa.

It was in DR Congo that I visited two of the most dangerous rebels in prison awaiting trial for war crimes. General Mateso Nyinga, known as Kung Fu, and Col Drati Massasi, known as Dragon. These men stood accused of killing more men, women and children than you could count.

It just so happened that the day I was meant to meet them fell on my birthday. Having spent twelve birthdays in prison, up until the age of thirty-two, through a miscarriage of justice, I never in my wildest dreams thought I'd be inside on the day of my 40th. The irony.

The prison guards wore uniforms and clutched weapons, but showed no interest in security. They didn't even rise from their white plastic chairs to pat me down. If they had, they may have found the small digital camera in my pocket. Investigators for the United Nations had been to see these men before I'd arrived there. They were following information they'd been given from witnesses, that Pakistani Peacekeepers had returned decommissioned weapons to these rebels. In a report, the UN had conducted inquiries to identify credible evidence, but concluded that they were unable to locate any witnesses who had seen the Peacekeepers in action. The report went on to say that during interviews with the UN investigators, Kung Fu and Dragon denied receiving weapons or ammunition from those Pakistani Peacekeepers. Two months before this report was made public, the rebels had issued a statement admitting that they had in fact been given weapons from the Peacekeepers.

The UN investigators did not go back to question the rebels to establish why they had changed their evidence. So, I did. Inside the prison compound, it was hard to tell the difference between prisoner and visitor. Chickens and goats wandered aimlessly in the dust, as men, women and children tended to small plots of grass from which they grew what they could. I was led unprotected, to the higher security complex where I was introduced to Floribert Njabu, president of the FNI militia group. The ethnic Lendu militia was involved in bitter clashes with their Hema rivals in the Ituri district of eastern DR Congo during the long war there. Njabu led me through a corridor of men, into the cell complex guarded by high concrete walls. The walk to meet Kung Fu and Dragon was not an easy one. For one, the smell of sewage mixed with sweat from the prisoners, clogged your nostrils, and the scent of alcohol was powerful. More importantly, these men were killers and most of those we passed were former rebels capable of barbaric crimes. At the end of a narrow concrete corridor, with little light coming in through barred windows, I was introduced to commander Kung Fu, and then Dragon. Their eyes were deep red, burnt by the coal they burned to cook food. Thousands of civilians lost their lives when these rebel leaders were in command. If what they confessed to me for the first time, in a recorded interview, from the confines of a prison cell is true, the reputation of Pakistani Peacekeepers and the UN would be damaged beyond repair. When I finished the interview and was leaving, a small entourage of FNI rebel commanders and ex-combatants slowly walked behind the footsteps of Njabu, their president, as he escorted us to an invisible point. We were told we could not go beyond it.

I returned to safety with all of the evidence I needed to complete the programme and bring the situation to light. During my career, there were two pivotal moments for the BBC in terms of storytelling. One was the Andrew Gilligan Story. He was accused by Alastair Campbell and Tony Blair of misquoting, and that blew up while I was at the Today Programme. The other story was when Jimmy Savile's paedophilia was exposed. Panorama had covered the story, which caused an explosion of controversy for the BBC.

I hadn't stopped going above and beyond for the BBC. I took huge risks, but I also reaped the rewards, for me and for my station. But this was all about to come to an end. James Harding joined the BBC in 2015 as the Head of News and Current Affairs, with the remit of shaking things up and swinging the axe. That he did.

There had only been four of us: John Sweeney, Paul Kenyon, Shelley Jofre and myself. But they decided to dissolve all the reporters' positions on Panorama. That marked the end of what I would consider a very challenging, but successful journalism career at the BBC. 2016 rolled by and, although I was reporting on The One Show and being offered other positions within the BBC, I didn't want to do it anymore. It's an elitist institution that systematically discriminates against people of colour, women and people from regional locations. I felt that the BBC had leached on my blood, sweat and sleepless nights in the same way that prison did.

I was forced to leave the BBC in the end, without so much as a thank you or a card. I was angry that Panorama was losing its way, I always thought that reporters made the show because we offered something different. It was also quite a scary time to be out of work. I now had kids, a mortgage, and that empty feeling I'd been covering up with work since my release, remained. I did the only thing I knew to do when unsure. I looked for a way forward. I became proactive in contacting production companies. I got myself an agent, and they were able to set me up a meeting with a production company called Emporium. I met with the managing director, and we spoke about doing a program around prison and crime. Channel

Five had commissioned Emporium to do "Inside the World's Toughest Prisons". They had already made one series with a presenter called Paul Connelly, the success of which attracted Netflix. However shortly after it moved to the streaming platform, the series was subject to criticism. The audience felt it was inauthentic and exaggerated. They needed to find a way of changing it, and fast.

I thought they were crazy when they first asked me to present. I had spent twelve years in prison unwillingly, and now someone wanted me to go and spend seven days in a cell, willingly? They must have been off their heads.

But then I thought long and hard about it. I had nothing else going on. I'd just gone through what felt like a divorce with the BBC, and I was still processing that. This is important to understand. This change was something I had to come to terms with – I'd spent twelve long years in one institution. Then, literally nine months after leaving it, I dove head-first into another: the BBC. Prison caused me psychological, physical, and emotional damage, and severely so. I had never had anything to help me address these issues. I became emotionally unstable, and it was only during this time, after the BBC, that I first sought out therapy. In those conversations with my therapist, it occurred to me that I had never truly dealt with the leftovers of the trauma which being wrongly convicted at twenty-years-old brought. When Netflix offered me this position, I realised what I had sitting in my lap. This experience would be another kind of therapy. I would go back to prison and see that there are others in the same position that I has been, that others were suffering in different places all around the world. I would get one step closer to closure.

PORTO
VELHO PRISON

" IF MY PERSONAL
JOURNEY HAS OPENED
YOUR EYES TO WHAT IS
HAPPENING TODAY IN OUR
OWN COUNTRY RIGHT
NOW, AND ALSO AROUND
THE WORLD, I INVITE YOU
TO TAKE ACTION. "

Chapter 11

Porto Velho Prison

Filming started inside the infamous Porto Velho Prison. Ahead of the trip, I was provided with YouTube videos and background briefings about the place and the kinds of prisoners that I would come face to face with. This was no joke.

Before my eyes moved footage detailing events that had only happened a few months prior to my arrival there. Even if I hadn't watched those videos, it was all over the news at the time. There had been prison riots. In the videos, I watched prisoners kicking the severed heads of other prisoners. Apparently, the whole thing had been triggered by a rivalry between two factions of gangs, the Red Command and the PCC, both involved with the drug trade both inside and outside the prison. We're talking about some eight to fifteen individuals who had their heads removed from their bodies. The prisoners I was due to meet would've been the ones involved in either the kicking of the heads, cutting off the heads, or sitting there watching and laughing while others participated in the decapitating of rival gang members. Nothing can prepare you for that.

Putting all of my fears aside, I travelled to Brazil. It was my first visit there. The journey to Porto Velho prison is convoluted because it's in Rondônia, North East of Brazil, tucked away in what you can only describe as the middle of nowhere. We were on a route there that was primarily used by South American drug cartels to transport drugs through

Brazil into other parts of the world. In recent years, the issue became a lot closer to home, with a lot of the drugs now being consumed locally.

It's not a tourist destination and there are very few foreigners. Nobody speaks English, they all speak their indigenous tongue, so if it hadn't been for my interpreter, I'd have had no way of communicating. When we got there, we were told that the hotel we were staying was the closest to the prison. It was a comfortable stay. Just as well because we weren't to leave the hotel under any circumstances. If we did, we would be putting ourselves in danger. In this remote region, any foreigner stands out and could easily become a target. The only place I was able to go to from the hotel, against all advice, was the local shops up the road. I knew the risk, but I couldn't take being cocooned in a hotel without any proper security. I had to get out. Often, after a day's shoot, I'd wander out of the hotel and up the road, about three or four hundred yards, and go into a shop. People would stare at me. They didn't see many Westerners come by, speaking English and buying a bar of chocolate, but that was about as much as I was able to do during the two weeks that I was there.

Although very gruesome, I needed to have watched the YouTube videos that I had. The prison had a culture of extreme violence, and I needed to know the danger I was in for. Better yet, I needed to know the code. I learned that, in addition to the two main factions, the Red Command and the PCC, prisoners who were not affiliated with either group were known as neutrals.

On the first day of shooting, we travelled to the location in a small white crew bus. It was a bleak place, surrounded by desert. We arrived at the prison, ready to behold a building as grandiose as the place's reputation. Turned out, it was nothing more than a crumbling mound made of brick and barbed wire.

I had a small team with me. It consisted of a local guy from Sao Paolo who was our 'fixer' and negotiated access, helping smooth the way for us. I had two camera people, neither of whom had been into a prison before. They had arrived in advance and done a 'recce' to get the lay of the land. They'd met with the director of the prison, talked to some of the guards, and even some of the prisoners, just to give them a vague heads-up about why we were coming and what it was all about. It was the best way to make sure they're all happy to take part, and it can save a lot of time on the first day of shooting.

Ahead of going into the prison, I went and met with the local police's Brazilian gangs task force, and that blew my mind! I turned up at the police headquarters, and there were hundreds of police officers lined up, ready to go on a street raid. They wanted to show me what the challenges were like in the outside world. After this, we tried to do something similar in all of the documentaries. It offered a rare insight into what life is like in the local community, and what types of people end up going to prison. In Brazil, they have a zero-tolerance drug policy. Anybody caught with any amount of cannabis or hashish or any drug would automatically go to prison. It doesn't matter who they are, what they've got, or what they've previously done.

We went on this high-speed siren blazing, gun-toting, expedition with the police. The ride was quite hairy, to put it mildly! When we reached the location, the police jumped out of their cars, guns pointed in all directions, only to find that the people they were targeting had already dispersed. Hardly surprising, as the blaring noise of the sirens may have given them a clue as to what was coming for them!

There was shouting coming from every which way, adrenalin levels through the roof. I jumped out of the van, wearing a police helmet and a bulletproof vest. The helmet tilted and covered my eyes because it was too big, so I ran blindly out of the van, trying to keep up with the police, as the cameramen followed suit.

It's impossible to know what kind of scenario you're going to find yourself in. One of these targets could, themselves, be in possession of a gun or a weapon, hence the bulletproof vest and helmet. However, on this occasion, they only made some small arrests of some very minor offenders, who were put in the back of the bus and taken in. They might not have ended up in a prison at first, but eventually, they would have wound up either in the one I was locked in, or another not too far away. A couple of days later, I made the same journey, to put myself in their shoes.

I decided in advance that, when I went into any prison, I'd wear a kind of uniform. To me that meant a black T-shirt, and a black pair of jogging bottoms or a black pair of shorts, and a pair of trainers. Throughout the series, you'll see that I'm always generally in black. There are two reasons for that. One, it's easy for me to buy ten black T-shirts that I could swap out after they got soaked with sweat (some of these countries were really hot and you could get salt stains on your clothes just from the sweat) and, two, because the colour black did a pretty good job of hiding those. Then there was also the matter of consistency and continuity for filming. Those were the reasons for the uniform. I won't lie, it also made me look a bit slimmer when I'd put on a bit of weight, as they say black does!

In this particular prison, the inmates were not given clothes on arrival and could wear what they liked, so I got to debut my uniform.

The first day of filming in Porto Velho Prison finally arrived. I got off the bus, and as we were about to go inside, I felt my pulse quicken and sweat started dripping from my skin under the hot Brazilian sun. The moment that I arrived, I was taken off our crew bus. It had been organised for me to be treated like any other prisoner. I was cuffed, and placed in the back of a prison bus to start my journey the same way any other prisoner would. Every guard was to ignore the fact that I was the host and presenter of a programme, who hadn't really committed a real crime in Brazil, and I was to receive no special treatment.

This prison was like nothing I'd ever experienced before. They were incredibly merciless. They made me strip down to nothing before they searched me thoroughly. All the while I was kept in handcuffs. They had allowed me to put my boxer shorts back on with my hands tied behind my back, which wasn't an easy task. After that, they took me into another space, where I was made to get onto my knees.

Throughout this entire time, the prison guards held assault rifles pointed towards me. It was during these moments that I'd take the opportunity to ask questions. Luckily, they'd been briefed to expect it, or I would have been shot for disobedience. I asked the guards why they needed to be so rough. They explained to me that they didn't know whether they were dealing with someone who was highly trained in martial arts, who could disarm them in seconds, or a more amateur prisoner. They had had prisoners enter their gates who were extremely dangerous, and had huge influence, and it was always a possibility that they had already corrupted other prison officers. So what they did to process these prisoners, was deemed necessary.

I was then taken into a big cell, where I was made to face a wall. My hands were still cuffed behind my back, but by now I'd at least managed to pull back on my boxer shorts. Two guards watched over me in this big, concrete space, while other guards stood further behind with a dog. At no point was I allowed to turn and face the guards. It was made clear from the very beginning, that I must not look the guards in the eye and should keep my eyes to the ground at all times. I took the opportunity to ask why. Apparently, most of the guards there didn't want to be recognised by the prisoners because it endangered their lives. I've never experienced anything like that. It was eerie to think that the threat to these guards was so concerning to them, that they would not allow prisoners to so much as lift their heads. So I walked around the whole time with my head down, my chin almost touching my chest.

Whilst I was facing the wall, the guard who stood behind me bombarded me with a barrage of questions. Do I take drugs? What gang am I from? Do I have any tattoos? What religion am I? What crime did I commit? They needed to know if I belonged to any gang, so they could decide where I'd end up in the prison. Intimidation set in. The guard made me drop my shorts again and squat. He made me cough to make sure there was nothing plugged up my bottom. When you cough, anything hidden up there would be forced out.

Once I had gone through all of this, I was taken to another part of the prison, where I was then questioned again by yet another guard. This is where I had my first interaction with other Brazilian prisoners. A number of us were sat on a bench.

We were all hand-cuffed behind our backs, wearing nothing but boxers, our heads down and looking at the ground. A lot of them had tattoos, or had big muscles or were very skinny, a sign that they were drug users. Nobody said a word to the other; I looked just like one of them. I think it was my skin colour. I could've passed as a Brazilian.

I was asked if I belonged to any gang, a vital question, because if they put me into the wrong space with the wrong faction, I could lose my life. I made sure they knew I was a neutral. It wasn't until this entire process was over, that I was uncuffed and given back my shorts and T-shirt. An officer handed me some bedding, and I was escorted to what would become my dormitory, which was shared with other prisoners. The set-up of the prison was quite unbelievable. Where I was staying wasn't the maximum-security area, but a sort of medium level, and despite there being no guards and no prison officers, there stood, looking over us, a watchtower always equipped with armed guards holding rifles.

The different factions were divided by two simple walls and housed in what they called pavilions. Within each pavilion, were individual houses and cells. The cells held ten to fifteen prisoners, but if you had influence or were high up in a hierarchy, then you might be in a cell which held just two or three. Many little cats ran around your ankles, and the smell was terrible. It was your real Latin American prison, overcrowded, crumbling brickwork and prisoners wandering around with no tops, in just shorts and flip flops. In the dusty exercise-yard, a few guys were kicking a football about.

What happened next was the beginning of one of the most important moments of the entire series. I was introduced to one particular guy, who was to be my chaperone. He was going to show me the ropes, and take me to meet my cell-mates. I was very aware that I was invading their space by bringing cameras in, so I had to respect that. Some were curious, while others displayed animosity towards me. Anything could happen behind locked doors. It was just me, and the two camera guys who filmed as much as they could, from whatever angles. None of us could know in advance what would happen, so I told the crew to keep the cameras rolling throughout so that we don't miss any important moments and interactions.

I was still quite terrified about everything that was going on. I was in this space now, with these guys, and there were no guards, or anyone else, around to watch out for us. I was entrusted to a prisoner I had only just met and knew nothing about. I knew from the beginning that I had to build trust and rapport with these prisoners. Two obvious obstacles stood in my way of doing that. The first was that I was not part of their gang. The second, that I didn't speak their language. Trying to convey a level of honesty and transparency with guys that already distrusted me, was not going to be easy. It took a long conversation for them to get to know me and what my intentions towards them were.

I sat on the end of a bed and let them interrogate me. They wanted to find out who I was and what I was doing there. Some of those men were high on drugs. Most of them were in for murder or another serious offence. They also would've been involved in the riots I mentioned earlier, where heads were chopped off and kicked around. The guy that was leading this informal interrogation later told me that decapitation wasn't the only thing to happen during those riots. Opposite his cell, there were seven prisoners locked in by one of the factions. They all burned to death. He'd seen it with his own two eyes. He was lucky to have been known as a neutral prisoner, otherwise, he also would have been attacked. He could smell their burning bodies from where he stood and could see the smoke rising through the bars. It was such a horrible and harrowing story, yet he managed to tell it to me in a most direct, unemotional way. I couldn't tell whether that meant I was earning trust, or not.

Their prodding questions naturally led to the moment I had to share that I was not a real prisoner. I told them that I was there to experience what their life was like, and to share with the world what they chose to share with me. I also told them that I'd been to prison myself. That brought about a complete change in atmosphere for all the prisoners. I was one of them. Then the real questions came. "What was it like?" "What were you in for?" I explained that I was in for murder and robberies. This won me a collective cheer from them. I told them that I had been in prison for twelve years, and they gave me a high five. They asked me if I shot the man or stabbed him. They wanted every last gory detail. The ice was broken. I was afraid I might end up ruining it all if I eventually told them that I'd been wrongly convicted. I explained that I never should have been imprisoned. Their admiration wasn't going anywhere. They showed me I was accepted in all the ways they could, friendly nudges and fist bumps went all round. At one point they put it into words, "You're one of us, man, you're one of us".

What followed next was such a powerful moment in the film, that lots of people have commented on it since. One of the prisoners asked me a very potent question. He said to me, "Having been sentenced to twelve years in prison, for a crime you didn't commit, didn't you think about taking your own life and killing yourself?" I turned around to him and answered, "No". I went on to tell that it had the opposite effect. It made me stronger, and more determined. It made me angry. It made me want to fight and claw my way out of where they had put me. I was not about to give in. This comment has resonated with so many people, that many wrote to me. I remember that one note explained that when they watched the film, they were in a dark place themselves, but when they heard me talk about the strength that my situation gave me to fight for justice, it gave them the strength to cope with their own situation. In some cases, helping them to think twice about suicide.

This one powerful question not only had long-term ramifications that stretched far beyond the TV series, but it also turned the tide for me and the prisoners, as they came to embrace me. Where they first warmed to me because they thought I was a murderer and a robber, now I had earned their respect. They realised I was a strong person individually. I could see that that's all they wanted to be themselves. Yes, they may have all been tough on the outside, they were killers and dealers and drug users, who had been hardened by the world they were in, even before they stepped foot into the prison. But when they found out about my story, I saw their body language change. They stopped to take a breath, and to think, telling themselves that if I had survived such a massive miscarriage of justice for twelve long years, then they could survive their own circumstances as well. The trust that this moment built, endured my entire stay in the prison. They'd sent word around the prison that I wasn't part of any gang, but that I was still one of them. People who weren't willing to talk to me, now opened up as if I was a friend.

They were prepared to share the stories about the horrors they had witnessed in the prison, and their lives.

One of these stories came from a particular prisoner who I met. I could tell by his wounds that he had been involved with the recent riots, and there had been a serious attempt on his life. It turned out that he was one of the instigators. As you'd expect, I had mixed feelings about meeting him. Still, I listened to his side of the story. As previously mentioned, the two main factions in the prison intermingled. It was an ongoing armed truce, but it never took much for hostilities to break out. On this occasion, it was the murder of a gang member from one faction, by the hand of a prisoner from the other. The guy I was talking to was part of the gang involved with the initial murder. Unsurprisingly, rival prisoners had then tried to kill him and, because the guards stay well away, it got out of hand. Later on, when I was doing chores as a cleaner, I came across a recessed cupboard area, with a secure barred and padlocked door on it. It contained the group of prisoners who had tried to kill him. The six of them had been segregated and locked away for their own safety.

The guys' heads poked out of the bars as they looked at me. If they all laid on the floor at once, there wouldn't have been enough space for them all to sleep. I asked them what they were doing there. The main guy lifted off his Brazilian football shirt and showed me his stab wounds. He told me that he was around when the riots took place and that people had tried to kill him. But he had survived. Now he just wants to get out to safety, because some of the guys in there were hell bent on revenge. I started to ask these men what was behind the violent culture in this prison. It was eye-opening to say the least, as you'll see when watching the programme for yourself.

Another profound moment on the show for me, was when I spent a day with the prison guards. I wanted to see what life was like for them and look at the whole situation through their eyes. When I arrived in the prison for the first time and was handed over to the officers, it had been the last time I had had any interaction with the guards. I had not seen them since then and still didn't have the slightest idea about what their duties and challenges were like.

I joined them first thing in the morning as they unlocked the cells for the first time since lockdown the night before. Last thing at night, padlocks are put on each cell and taken off first thing in the morning. The infrastructure of the prison was the ricketiest thing I'd ever seen. If you leant on the wall, it would probably collapse. The only thing that kept the order, was that the prisoners knew they'd be shot without warning if they made any attempt to escape. In the month before I arrived, many a prisoner had been shot dead by the authorities. They make a lesson out of them.

As I followed a group of prison guards around each Pavilion to unlock cells, I noticed that each one was carrying either an assault rifle or a shotgun. Every time we approached the pavilion, the guards got out their guns and loaded them as loudly as they could before they approached the entrance. Most of the guards had pulled balaclavas down over their faces to avoid the prisoners identifying them, which gave them a rather menacing appearance. They were a fearsome sight. All of the prisoners stood back, away from the cell doors, as they were being unlocked. Once unlocked, nobody moved, and nobody went to leave their cells. It didn't make any sense to me. Normally, in other prisons, the guards would unlock the cell doors and the prisoners would walk out right away.

What I witnessed was that each prisoner waited for all of the doors to be unlocked, before daring to step out. The guards then retreated backwards as a group, still brandishing their weapons. Only once they had retreated to at least twenty yards did the prisoners move. It was like a stand-off. They told me that it was a rule that no prisoner could come within twenty metres of a guard. If they did, then they would be shot.

From that moment on, for the rest of the day until lockdown, the guards would move into their area, where they could observe the prisoners from a distance. The same process would happen in reverse later in the evening. At mealtimes, it was left to the trusted prisoners to collect and serve meals. I'd been there a few days now, and luckily nobody had threatened me or the team that I was working with. That just served as a reminder of just how dangerous this environment was.

There was only really one moment which had the potential of getting ugly. At the beginning of the filming process, when I was meeting the first group of prisoners who would become my cell-mates, there were other prisoners outside of that particular dormitory, listening and watching. My sixth sense told me that they were not happy about what was going on, jealous that I was getting on so well with their fellow inmates, and felt left out. I could tell by their body language and their facial expressions, and the whispering that was going on. I know from experience what it feels like to be left out, and my concern was that they would poison the minds of the other prisoners and turn them against us, a recipe for disaster. The only way I managed to snuff out the risk posed to us, was by going over there and involving them. In order to build trust with them, I offered to help work on their daily chores. I found myself cleaning the toilets, some very shitty toilets, and equally dirty shower areas. The last thing I wanted was to become the target of a kidnapping or hostage-taking. Prisoners can be very clever and cunning about turning a situation in their favour and using it to seek attention. By defusing the situation, I was introduced to a couple more prisoners who had some very powerful stories to share.

There were three sections of the prison that I spent time in. In addition to the Pavilion I was in, there was a studio which was a maximum, maximum security area, where the worst of the gang members were isolated. It was a vile space, consisting of thick concrete and bars. I met some of the young gang members who were being kept in there, and no matter what they had done, no one deserved to be trapped in such a terrible place.

The third and final space I spent time in was the rehabilitation section. I spent one day there. It turned out to be a most unusual and disturbing experience for me. I walked into a big gymnasium hall, to find that all of the prisoners were already there and all stripped down to their boxer shorts. An instructor was encouraging them to make funny noises and be outlandish, in a bid to help them release pent-up anger. It was designed to be some sort of free-style hybrid of a yoga class/ relaxation session. I tried my best and got stuck in with all the noise-making and exercises. I was like a kid, pretending to be a jungle animal. Once it was over, we all stepped out of the gym, where there were two lines of prisoners, each holding a big bucket of what I can only describe as mud scented, with lemongrass. It was a tradition to add a hallucinogenic to the mud, although on this occasion, they assured me that there was none. One of the prisoners in front of me took a huge scoop of mud and started to lather my body with it. I won't lie, it was strange. It was the first time another man had touched me in such a way. He covered my face, my hair, my neck, my shoulders, all the way down my body, carefully avoiding my private parts. The mud dried all over my body, and if I thought I'd looked fresh out the jungle before, this was a whole new level. Just when I thought it was all finally over, I found out that it was my turn to spread the mud on a fellow prisoner. The man stood there patiently, waiting. This was even more uncomfortable; it was the first time in my life that I was touching another man's body.

When the ritual came to an end, it only seemed right to have a chat with the guys. The first thing that I found out totally shocked me. The person whose hands had been all over my body was a convicted murderer and a rapist. It just felt so strange. Looking at his hands, these were hands that had raped. These were hands that had killed. These were the hands that had just rubbed mud all over my body. Although I continued to question him about his crimes, I couldn't shake the icky feeling it had given me.

They then threw buckets of rainwater onto us to wash all the mud off. It should have been a nice experience, but that rainwater smelled terrible. The only saving grace was that it had everyone laughing and smiling together. For a split second, although we didn't speak the language, I was able to communicate with them without needing to call on the translator. It was a restorative end to what had been seven days with some of the most intense and petrifying prisoners, in one of the most barbaric prisons that I've ever experienced. In some of the later programmes, I came across some that were nearly just as bad, but the people were never nearly as brutal as the prisoners in Porto Velho.

When I was released from Porto Velho, I bid my farewells to the prisoners I had met and built up bonds with. They'd confided in me because I took the time to listen to their stories, and this kind of connection isn't a superficial one.

On reflection on my time there, I believe that most of them had lost hope. There was no end in sight for them and no real rehabilitation. It was a place where prisoners went to lose their lives, and they didn't value those of their fellow inmates either. It was hell, and would always be so for them. I will never forget it. As it brought to an end the first episode of the Netflix series, 'Inside the World's Toughest Prisons', I told myself surely none could be as bad as this? I was soon to discover that, yes, yes they could! There were to be another six series to come, and with many more, very real adventures behind bars all around the world, which you'll be able to read about in the future.

Epilogue

At the very beginning of the book I questioned whether everything that happens to us helps to shapes the person we later become. For many years I did not see this. I was angry at the injustice I had received and took that anger out on the system and those who were implementing it. At no time did I ever give us and every setback I received made me stronger and more determined to see justice properly served.

Having had the powerful and challenging experiences that I have, it would be a waste if I didn't now channel them into achieving something positive and to help other people who are also going through a similar dark journey. Working in the media with the BBC and currently with Netflix, has given me a profile around the world and a voice. This was not something that I sought but it has happened nevertheless. It is a gift that has been given to me. If I have learned anything over the past two decades, both behind bars and in front of the camera, I have learnt that there is injustice everywhere.

I have learnt that the truth on its own isn't enough, and sometimes you have to fight for it.

I have learnt that society can be unforgiving and prejudiced and that those people in a position to judge others are not always impartial and can have agendas of their own.

I have learnt that we all need to be more vigilant to protect the values that hold us together as a society and not to prejudge anyone without listening to both sides of the story.

I have learnt that my work is now only just beginning and that all my many experiences have indeed been for a purpose and I believe that that is to shine a light into dark places and ask those probing questions that only a journalist can.

However, one voice is not enough to make a real difference. If I am to do anything to fight in-justice and to speak for those who are not in a position to speak for themselves, I need help. This is why I am currently setting up the Raphael Rowe Foundation.

"The mission of the Raphael Rowe Foundation is to champion injustice and to inspire those who administer the prison systems throughout the world, to abolish dehumanising, degrading and dangerous practices and to put more emphasis on the mental health and safety of those in their care."

I am looking for people who are not willing to remain silent where silence condones the unacceptable.

I am looking for people who want a fairer society which respects the human right of everyone, irrespective of the mistakes they may have made in their lives.

I am looking for people who have been moved by the inhuman and degrading conditions that far too many people have to endure behind bars. Serving time in prison to make amends to society for committing a crime should be just that. It should not mean having their lives being put in danger or being dehumanised. That was never part of the sentence that was handed down. As a society and as caring individuals, what are we prepared to accept being done in our name?

If my personal journey has opened your eyes to what is happening today in our own country right now, and also around the world, I invite you to take action.

Please visit my website, www.raphael-rowe.com where you will find more information about current issues that need to receive the glare of publicity and also ways that you can add your voice to mine in helping to bring about positive change.

I can't do this alone, but together we can make a difference

Thank you

Lightning Source UK Ltd.
Milton Keynes UK
UKHW020654070221
378373UK00006B/37